FROM THE FILES

THE ROYAL ENGINE

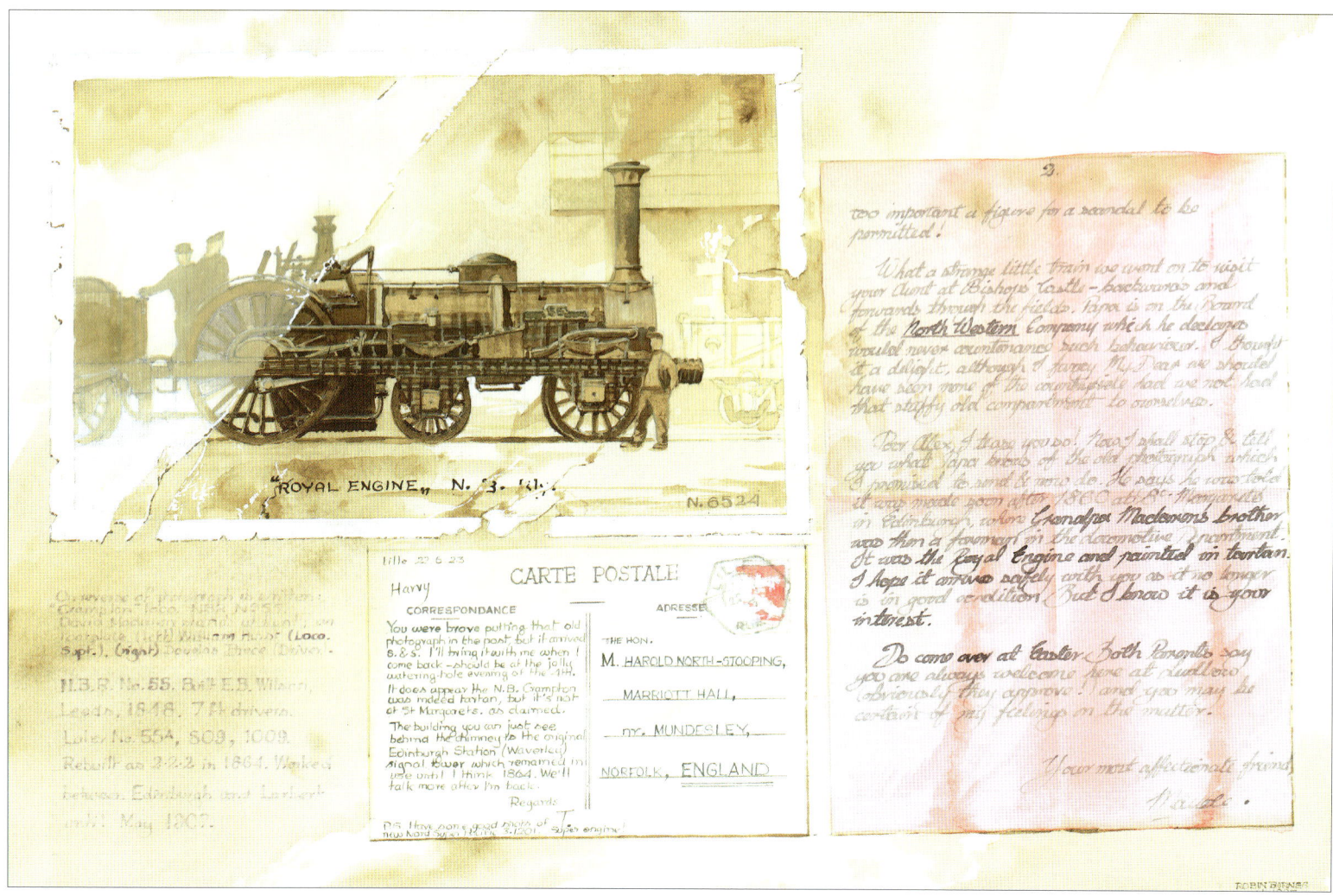

In 1848 E.B. Wilson of Leeds completed a group of six Crampton 4-2-0 locomotives, five of which went to the Eastern Counties Railway and one, pictured, to the North British as its No.55. A well constructed and fast running locomotive known to footplatemen as 'Deersfoot', it nonetheless had a life in this form of only seven years, succumbing to the poor standards of maintenance then prevailing in the upkeep both of track and rolling stock. The NBR did have an official Royal Engine, No.57 *The Queen*, built by Hawthorn, but it was of inferior build quality and rode badly. It is not unlikely the story is correct, that following the opening on 29 August 1850 of the Royal Border Bridge at Berwick-upon-Tweed, it was No.55 that was chosen to bring Queen Victoria on to Edinburgh. It is believed also that on the day it was painted almost overall in the Royal Stewart tartan. The fact this went unmentioned in the local press is not significant, for then locomotives on such prestigious duty had the appearance of having run amok through a garden centre and commonly were so over-dressed with shrubbery, banners and busts that what was beneath would have been scarcely visible (A former NBR engineer, in later years resident in India, stated he had known a St. Margarets' chargehand, present at the time, who had confirmed to him that No.55 was so painted). On the front of the locomotive was a curved headboard proclaiming God Save The Queen, which Edinburgh wags suggested in reality was a reference to the current condition of the NBR tracks (for more on the Crampton type, see also Chapter 24).

FROM THE FILES

AN ARTIST LOOKS AT LOCOMOTIVE DEVELOPMENT

ROBIN BARNES

© ROBIN BARNES 2018

All rights reserved. No part of this publication may be reproduced, stored in a retrieval system, or transmitted in any form or by any means, electronic, mechanical, photocopying, recording or otherwise without prior permission in writing from the publishers.

Robin Barnes asserts the moral right to be recognised as the author of this work.

British Library Cataloguing-in-Publication-Data:
a catalogue record of this book is held by the British Library.

First Printing 2018

ISBN No. 978-1-909358-42-3

Published in Great Britain by
Camden Miniature Steam Services
Rode, Frome, Somerset. BA11 6NZ

Camden stock and publish a wide selection of railway, transportation and engineering books;
see their full range at: www.camdenminm.co.uk

Layout and design by Andy Luckhurst, Trowbridge, Wilts.

Printed by Amber Book Print.

COVER ILLUSTRATIONS

Upper: Former Midland & South Western Junction Railway No.14 at work following extensive surgery by the North British Railway Cowlairs Works (Chapter 13).
Lower: A project that almost came to fruition, the Chapelon three-cylinder compound 2-10-4 of 1946 (Chapter 35).

CONTENTS

INTRODUCTION	2

PART 1 LOCOMOTIVES THAT WERE

CHAPTER

1	1814	BRUNTON LOCOMOTIVE	10
2	1856	PENNSYLVANIA RAILROAD Baldwin 4-4-0 No.134 Tiger	12
3	1858	EDINBURGH, PERTH & DUNDEE RAILWAY Train Ferry Carrier	14
4	1865	GREAT NORTHERN RAILWAY 400 Class 0-6-0 (steam tender)	16
5	1876	GRAZ KÖFLACHER BAHN 2-2-0T (inspection car)	18
6	1894	McCARY LOGGING COMPANY 0-6-0 (oscillating cylinder)	20
7	1906	NORTH EASTERN RAILWAY 4CC Class 4-4-2 No.731	22
8	1907	COMPAGNIE GÉNÉRALE des OMNIBUS, PARIS Purrey 0-4-0T (steam tram)	24
9	1907	WOLGAN VALLEY RAILWAY Vale & Co 2-2-0T (steam railbus)	26
10	1910	ÉTAT BELGE Type 36 2-10-0 No.4405	28
11	1910	REID-RAMSAY 2`B+2`B (steam turbine electric)	30
12	1916	ERIE RAILROAD 2-8-8-8-2 P1 Class No.2603 (Triplex type)	32
13	1916	NORTH BRITISH RAILWAY Beyer Peacock/Cowlairs 2-6-0	34
14	1918	NEW YORK, NEW HAVEN & HARTFORD RAILROAD GE/Alco 2`AA+AA2` No.068 (AC electric)	36
15	1920	VISIMU – UTKINSK RAILWAY Glover 2-8-0 КОММУНИСТ	38
16	1924	LONDON, MIDLAND & SCOTTISH RAILWAY Hookham 3F 0-6-0 No.2367	40
17	1929	DEUTSCHEN VERSUCHSANSTALT für LUFTFAHRT Propeller drive test vehicle	42
18	1931	LIMBURGSCHE TRAMWEG MAATSCHAPPIJ 0-6-0+0-6-0 No.51 (Garratt type)	44
19	1937	QUEENSLAND RAILWAYS Ipswich RM32 Endeavour (petrol engine rail motor)	46
20	1946	GULF, MOBILE & OHIO RAILROAD Model 4-S B-B No.1900 (diesel electric)	48
21	1947	GREAT NORTHERN RAILWAY (Ireland) McIntosh U Class 4-4-0 No.205 Down	50
22	1948	FC NATIONAL GENERAL BELGRANO Porta 4-8-0 Argentina	52
23	1953	EGYPTIAN STATE RAILWAYS Jung B+B (diesel mechanical)	54

INTERLUDE: TRAMS	56
CENTREPIECE: BELGIAN FANCIES	58

PART 2 LOCOMOTIVES THAT WEREN'T

CHAPTER

24	1856	HESSISCHE LUDWIGSBAHN Maschinenfabrik Esslingen 4-2-0 (Crampton type)	62
25	1874	HURD & SIMPSON 0-6-0WT (underground locomotive)	64
26	1889	MALLET-BRUNNER 2-4-2 (two-cylinder compound)	66
27	1894	CHASE-KIRCHNER (Aerodromic System)	68
28	1918	LANCASHIRE & YORKSHIRE and CALEDONIAN Railways Hughes 2-10-0 and Pickersgill 2-10-2	70
29	1929	LIMA LOCOMOTIVE WORKS Woodard 2-12-6	72
30	1930	LONDON & NORTH EASTERN and LONDON, MIDLAND & SCOTTISH Railways LNER Doncaster and Beyer Peacock/LMS Bo-Bo (diesel electric)	74
31	1932	HARLAND & WOLFF 4-6-0-0-6-4 (diesel electric)	76
32	1935	GENERAL ELECTRIC/GREAT LAKES AIRCRAFT COMPANY Aircraft (high pressure steam, turbine propulsion)	78
33	1940	SOUTHERN RAILWAY Bulleid 4-6-0	80
34	1943	LONDON, MIDLAND & SCOTTISH RAILWAY Coleman 2F 0-6-0	82
35	1946	SOCIÉTÉ NATIONALE des CHEMINS de FER FRANÇAIS Chapelon 152P 2-10-4	84
36	1948	ROMNEY, HYTHE & DYMCHURCH RAILWAY Hunter 4-4-4-4 (Duplex type)	86
37	1987	DEUTSCHE REICHSBAHN (DDR) Wendler 2`C (Fireless type)	88

POSTSCRIPT: STEAM'S LAST DAYS	90
VALETE: THE CULPRIT	92

INTRODUCTION

A BIOGRAPHICAL NOTE

The boy had settled at his favourite spot, in the long grass of the bank that sloped down from canal to railway just to the west of Falkirk High, a station situated on the busy former LNER Edinburgh to Glasgow main line. 'High' truly it was, for from where he sat he could see northward clear across the town of Falkirk to the River Forth and the barrier formed by the Ochil Hills, a panoramic sweep that in its way encapsulated almost the entire history of industrial Scotland. Directly north, by Stenhousemuir, stood the iron foundries of the Carron Company, its blast furnaces first tapped in 1760, in its heyday a centre of innovation and one of the largest works of its kind in Europe. Here in 1801 and 1803 had been assembled the engines of two steam-powered tow boats, both carrying the same name, Charlotte Dundas, and both tried on the Forth & Clyde Canal, the second regarded as the first successful example of its kind. That same waterway, fifteen years later, was to see also the world's first practical iron ship, the Passage Boat Vulcan, built by Thomas Wilson and two blacksmiths, drawn by teams of horses and able to carry up to 150 passengers in some comfort. Close by the foundries, on the Forth & Clyde Canal, were the premises of the British Aluminium Company and the Falkirk Corporation gas works, while off to the east lay the great timber ponds of Grangemouth. Beyond stood the epitome of modern industry, the growing petrochemical complex, not long recommissioned following its World War 2 shut down. It was a familiar view, one that imbued in him a lasting love of industrial landscapes. Only in later life did the awareness come that behind them lay hard toil, danger and often exploitation. Also at Grangemouth, although it had not then properly registered on the boy's consciousness, stood what had been intended as a home for civil aviation, the Central Scottish Airport. When opened in May 1939 it was already a substantial affair with control tower and two large hangars, but was quickly expanded, in part as a base for RAF fighters, though largely as an Operational Training Unit. By this date, four years after the end of hostilities, it had become a gliding school and depot for RAF Maintenance Command (closure came in 1955).

It was hot, this mid-June day of 1949, and as it happened the boy's eighth birthday. Behind him the weed-grown surface of the Union Canal was undisturbed, commercial activity having ceased almost twenty years previously. Of the usually active pond life, this morning there was no sign. All of nature, it seemed, was taking its ease. In contrast, the man-made mechanical world immediately in front of him was busy as ever, a constant procession of trains passing back and forth before his gaze. Every one was in the charge of a steam locomotive, some large, others small, some old, others fresh from the erecting shop of the North British Locomotive Company in Glasgow. So many of the locomotives familiar to him in those days bore names, from the romantic – *Bantam Cock, Black Duncan, Irish Elegance, Lady of Avenel, Sayajirao, Sun Chariot* and *Wizard of the Moor* – to the truly prosaic – *Andrew K. McCosh* and *Harry Hinchcliffe*. There was little *Plumer* also, a regular on local goods workings. But there was a train, not a locomotive, which the boy made a point of looking out for, the Queen of Scots, 10.50am Glasgow Queen Street to London Kings Cross via Leeds. Shortly before 11.30, on schedule, it sped past, seven umber and cream Pullman carriages behind the engine, passengers at tables with individual lamps, part hidden by curtained windows, deferential attendants briefly glimpsed. Important people; what kind of world did they live in? What was it like? Far removed from any he would inhabit, or so he thought then, for he could not know that the following year the family would move to Scotland's capital and that exactly a decade later he would enter the world of civil aviation, one almost certainly beyond that experienced by the passengers in the Pullman. As the last echoes of the locomotive's whistle drifted from inside Falkirk High tunnel, the boy rose, dusting grass from his best trousers. Time to go; on no account was he to be late for his birthday party. He sighed. He liked birthdays, but parties were not really his thing.

The boy, of course, was the author. Growing up as he did surrounded by sights such as these, day in, day out, and the sounds associated with them, it was small wonder a fascination with railways and all their doings early on took a firm grip. And there was more. At no distance from the rear of the family home, its workings clearly visible across the intervening wheat field, stood Policy Colliery. Comparatively small, employing around one hundred men, nonetheless it boasted extensive sidings reached by a connecting line which climbed steeply behind Falkirk High station, crossed the Slamannan Road on the level, then climbed again via a reversing neck to the mine. An extension, a little under a mile in length ran southward through the fields to a brick works at Glen. Formerly owned by the Callendar Coal Company, in January 1947 the colliery had passed to the state, and an early memory is of watching as the rows of internal user wagons, their red paint faded to pink, over a short period of time were changed to a fresh pillar-box red, the company name in large white letters replaced by the initials NCB. On Sundays, with no-one around, an illicit visit would be paid to the two locomotives, one cold and held as spare, the other still warm from its Saturday morning shift, surrounded by the familiar aromas of coal-fired steam, of smoke, soot, hot ash, water and oil. Both were products of the famous Scottish maker, Andrew Barclay of Kilmarnock. The regular engine, Barclay's number 1981, was a youngster of just fifteen years, but the spare, its number 170, had first seen the light of

2

day in 1875. It had received a major repair in 1922, although was little altered in appearance. It looked old, with its ogee shape saddle tank, elegantly curved cab side sheets and large dumb buffers. What the enginemen thought of their veteran machine is unknown, but to this youthful observer it was a delight. In it almost certainly lay the beginning of a life-long interest, not simply in observing the unusual and obscure, but in recording it too, initially in the form of pencil sketches and later, from about 1960, also through photography. The camera has been a tool of research – no claim to photographic skill is made – but at least it was taken up in time to capture on film images of railway operation and industrial practices little changed in a century or more and on the brink of being swept away almost overnight by the tides of progress. The photograph of the little Avonside at windswept Millom is an illustration (See Postscript), as is (1), when in July 1964 the former Consett Iron Company B.No.23 (Hawthorn Leslie 3744/1929) smoked its way through the mid-day break at Seaham Harbour, County Durham. Ships, provided they had tall funnels, became an interest, an example being Lord Cochrane's Rising Star of 1821 (2), the first British-built steam warship, part sail and part propelled by a single internal paddle wheel. Intended for the Chilean navy, in practice it spent its life in merchant service along the Pacific coast of South America. Road vehicles feature hardly at all, unless powered by steam, and it was a pleasant surprise, on a murky day in August 1968, in the course of a visit to the Brown Bayley works in Sheffield, to find hard at work a fleet of Sentinel

3

steam lorries (3). They were not licensed for use on the public road, but employed internally carrying steel slabs and other items between departments. Steam railway locomotives have always been a major interest, reflected in the content of this book, but to an extent also have been other forms of motive power, particularly when of unusual arrangement, or of some rarity. Image (4) illustrates a design which was intended to be neither of these, instead a British Railways standard class. However through an unfortunate combination of mechanical unreliability and loss of the kind of traffic it was intended to work, in the end it became both. This was Clayton Equipment's Type 1 diesel-electric, 117 of which were constructed between 1962 and 1965, yet all of which had left normal service by the end of 1971. Here D8570 makes heavy weather of the climb away from Edinburgh on the old Caledonian main line one evening in May 1966. New in January 1964, less than six years later it had been reduced to scrap.

Railway rolling stock in general has proved less of an attraction, though with exceptions, amongst these the earliest British sleeping cars. One reason is that the first of all would have passed that favourite viewing point at Falkirk High, many years previously. Built for the North British Railway by the Ashbury Railway Carriage & Wagon Company, it entered service between Glasgow and London in April 1873, south and north bound on alternate nights. The internal arrangements may be seen in (5), there being two compartments each with three fold-down sleeping berths side by side, separated by a central compartment containing lavatory and water closet. The interior decoration, which seems hardly conducive to restful slumber, is shown inset at bottom right. The vehicle was not a success, possibly in part for this reason and in part because few British travellers then would have considered such intimacy acceptable, even if all concerned remained fully clothed (in North America, where very long journeys were commonplace, it was otherwise, but a combination of many layers of clothing, sleeping with boots on and lack of washing facilities tended to discourage the formation of the more intense kind of relationship). Two years later, in 1875, a partner company on the East Coast route, the Great Northern, attempted a form of sleeper, which even allowing for the fact that these were early days, seems quite extraordinarily inept. Described by the historian Cuthbert Hamilton Ellis as "probably the most barbarous sleeping-berth arrangement ever seen in a European train," it is illustrated at bottom left. In reality, it was no more than an adapted First Class compartment, the four 'berths' consisting of one full width seat and three padded boards, two laid across the exterior door spaces and one across the access to the water closet and lavatory, the passengers lying in a square, foot to face. If one of them required to use the facilities during the journey – very likely – then the unfortunate individual lying across that door would be forced to get up and lift his board out of the way.

Maltreatment of passengers by railway companies, whether it was real or supposed, was a godsend to cartoonist and satirist, and a wonderful resource for those interested is Punch magazine, especially during the 19th Century. The school library had a fine collection of bound volumes and latterly the author spent more time leafing through these than studies properly permitted, though it did result in an appreciation of the cartoonists' figure drawing skills, in particular their ability to convey a wide range of facial expressions in a naturalistic manner. The cartoons often were very funny and (6), rather later from 1927, is a favourite, here redrawn and slightly adapted. Of the Underground in London it wrote (1881); "The one duty of the Guard is to 'keep time.' He is not expected to keep anything else, except tips. For instance, he is not bound to keep his temper, or to keep a look out for Roughs." (Undesirables invading First Class compartments were a recurring problem.) The maze that was old Waterloo was regularly targeted by Punch's writers, who would describe how even the porters were unable to locate trains and of how posters displayed timetables for every railway company other than the London & South Western, to which concern, they would point out with relish, the premises belonged.

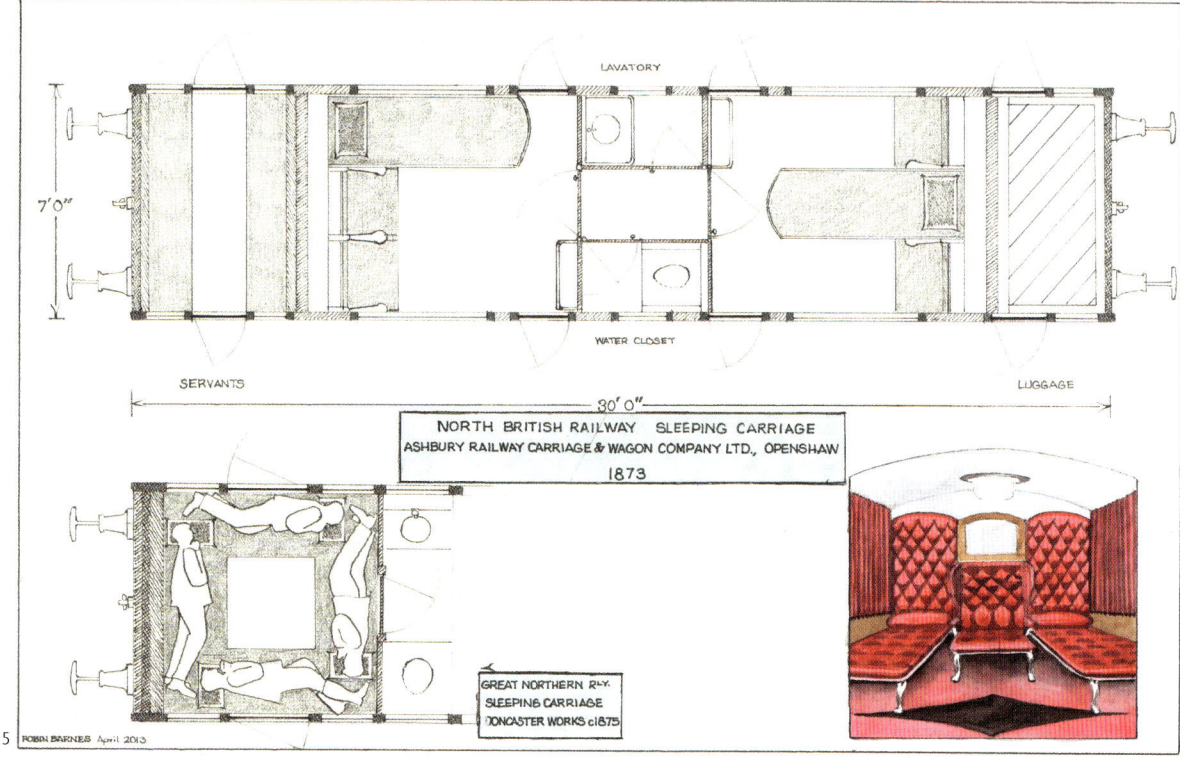

While the move to Edinburgh did little to diminish existing interests, it added another, in aviation. The new family home stood within clear view of the eastern approach and take off path of Turnhouse airfield's then main runway (today the vastly expanded Edinburgh Airport). In 1950 there was not only the first generation of military jet aircraft to be seen, but also stalwarts of the piston engine era, military and civil, in almost infinite variety. The field was home to No.603 City of Edinburgh Squadron, Royal Auxiliary Air Force, still flying the Spitfire, though only just, for in May 1951 it began to receive the jet Vampire FB5. On 1 July 1951, ten of the squadron's Spitfire F22s, in a salute to its new Honorary Air Commodore, Princess Elizabeth, and in farewell to the famous fighter, flew over the city in E formation, a sight which this young man found both moving and totally irresistible. Large formations of military aircraft, rare now, at the time remained commonplace in Britain's skies, and another outstanding memory of those early days in Edinburgh is of one cold but clear winter's afternoon in 1953. From the back garden of the family home a steady throbbing sound became audible, approaching from the south-east and gradually increasing in intensity until into view came a formation of fourteen giant United States Air Force ten-engine B36 bombers (six piston, four jet). They were not flying very high, or fast, probably not using their jet engines, and with wings spanning 236ft and fuselages over 160ft long, they filled the sky for what seemed more than just a few minutes (the author now understands the date probably was 13 February, the aircraft belonging to the 7th Bomb Group, en route from a detachment at RAF Fairford in Gloucestershire, via Goose Bay in Labrador, to their home base at Carswell, Texas). Such sights made a deep and lasting impression, yet what they represented, the possible extinction of the human race and much else besides, passed literally and figuratively above his head. Later that same year, during the annual RAF Turnhouse At Home event, crowds were treated to their first experience of an aircraft breaking the so-called Sound Barrier, when a Royal Canadian Air Force Sabre fighter dived steeply from a great height, creating an immensely satisfying double bang. To him, these were simply exciting times, and he would revel in the latest grainy photograph, or speculative artist's impression, of some new Soviet aircraft, "now known to be entering service," which usually it was not. In September 1958, during the Edinburgh International Festival, a full-size replica of the first US guided weapon to carry a nuclear warhead, the MGM5 Corporal tactical ballistic missile, was set up atop the Waverley Market, today's Mall (7). How bizarre, that a representation of such a massively destructive weapon of war should ever have been considered a suitable object for display as a part of an international arts festival.

Although first flights had been made in September 1954, a return trip between Renfrew and Ringway in a BEA Dakota, opportunities to fly in aircraft rather than simply watch them really began in 1957, with the RAF Section of the school Combined Cadet Force. There would be Saturday morning air experience in Chipmunk trainers out of Turnhouse, summer camps at operational airfields and field days, a particularly memorable occasion being in July 1957, when seated on the fuselage floor in two Avro Lincoln bombers the Section was transported to and from West Freugh, near Stranraer, in south-west Scotland. The twenty years from 1960 were spent in a non-flying rôle with the former British European Airways. Being based variously at Heathrow, Edinburgh and outstations afforded the author opportunities to sample a great variety of aircraft ranging from piston-engine old timers to the latest designs. Most notably perhaps, the early Soviet jet Tu104, based on the Tu16 bomber, with its net luggage racks, lace antimacassars, bakelite ashtrays and tricky steps up and down where the cabin floor was raised to permit the wing centre section to pass through. Also from Russia came the Ilyushin IL18, one of the more pleasant of the large turboprop aircraft in which to fly, while from the USA came the graceful Lockheed Super Constellation and rare Convair 990, the fastest of the earlier generation jet airliners. Unforgettable was the Super VC10, the airliner BOAC did not want, but which became a firm favourite with its passengers. Smooth and quiet inside, it was of typically robust British construction, able to fly in and out of hot and high airports with short runways, but more costly to operate than its American rivals. The airline did eventually realise just how popular the aircraft was and produced a memorable series of advertisements under the heading 'Try A Little VC Tenderness.' One recalls a giant poster on one of the platforms at Clapham Junction on which British United Airways promoted its VC10 services to East Africa. (8) pictures G-ASGH making a transit stop in Barbados at sunset on 24 February 1969, en route Port of Spain to Heathrow. It truly was a lovely aeroplane, its lines enhanced by what might be argued was the most stylish of all airline liveries (G-ASGH later served with the RAF, until broken up in 1987). The image was captured in the course of the flight home following time on the island of Trinidad, where it had been but a short hop to the palms and white sands of Tobago. The majority of flights between the two were in the hands of Viscount aircraft, but one service each morning was flown by a British West Indian Airways/Air Jamaica Boeing 727 on its way to New York. This called in briefly at Tobago, but the Boeing, too large for the small airport's taxiways, parked on the runway, where it is seen (9) in a photograph which captures both the fashions and relaxed atmosphere of the time.

An interest in railways that begins with engines and numbers as often as not over time will greatly broaden its scope. Railways, it may fairly be argued, made the modern world, and serious study of their history will lead the student into many other fields, of geography, geology, politics and finance, of civil and mechanical engineering. And if he or she wishes to seek them out, to be found also are foul deeds, of violence, general skulduggery and fraud, the last named sometimes on a massive scale. Other avenues might open; for example, a fascination with the streamlined steam locomotive in the USA pointed the author towards the Art Deco period and Modernism of the 1930s. In illustration 10, we see a fashionably dressed young woman, a 1936 Cord 810 saloon and the Pennsylvania Railroad's giant 304 ton 'Duplex', No.6100. Its external appearance was the work of the famous industrial designer Raymond Loewy, who at about the same time, demonstrating his versatility, brought the world the sleek Electrolux refrigerator. No.6100 in truth was too large for the job and was not repeated (but see Chapter 36), although the sight and sound of its passing, hauling a 1200 ton train at 100 mph, experienced at close quarters, would not have been easily forgotten. The glamour portrait, too, one might associate with Art Deco, although that would be mistaken, for its origin lies lost in the mists of time.

Arguably the best came from the brush of Peruvian born, naturalised American, Alberto Vargas (1896-1982), a master of watercolour and pastel. The showgirl Anna Mae Clift became a favourite model, his best friend and companion in a marriage which lasted forty-four years until her death in 1974, an event from which he is said never to have fully recovered. Though often finding much to admire in this kind of portraiture, in what might be described as its mid-20th Century pin-up incarnation, the author has not attempted its like other than in this image (11), the response to a challenge made some years ago, in which elements of Japanese and Western fashion styles were to be combined.

The author likes to think that his interest in rail transport is all embracing, but in truth it is dominated by the steam locomotive. That this is so is hardly surprising, because in Britain, diesel and electric traction, combined with radical changes to the railway infrastructure, did not really begin to alter the scene until he was out of his teenage years. He grew up through an age when other than in parts of the Scottish Highlands and remoter Wales, nowhere in the British Isles was far from the sound of the steam railway. For a long time it had been possible to pass from childhood to old age without there being real change. The sound of the train, near or distant, and the activity which surrounded it was a constant. It provided a sense of security, of continuity. It formed the bedrock almost upon which peoples' everyday existence was constructed. The child rousing from a troubling dream, the wife lying awake concerned for an absent husband, perhaps fighting for his country in some distant part, the sick and the elderly, all, as they lay, would hear beyond the window the familiar reassuring sounds. The 1936 documentary Night Mail captures well that comforting sense of timeless rhythm. The lines from W.H. Auden's accompanying poem which to the author capture this best are not perhaps those most widely remembered:

Sheep dogs cannot turn her course
They slumber on with paws across
In the farm she passes no-one wakes
But a jug in the bedroom gently shakes

This, then, forms the background to his interests, or at least some of them, the book a journey, as it were, down the less familiar branch lines of railway history, discovering along the way the interesting, the unusual and the downright strange. The first part looks at locomotives that did exist, and the second at unfulfilled projects. The latter appear to have been genuine proposals, put forward in all seriousness, though not necessarily so refined as to be intended as a definitive arrangement, ready for construction, but rather illustrating a step along the way. All images, drawn, painted or photographic, are the work of the author, and for their shortcomings he takes full responsibility, while every effort has been made to ensure the accuracy of the text. This, though, is no work of reference, but rather it is intended as food for the imagination, to be enjoyed at leisure. And the presence of ships, aircraft and people too? The title of this work permits it, for the dictionary defines locomotive as anything 'having power of moving from place to place.'

Robin Barnes
Edinburgh, Autumn 2017

Weights and measures given are generally those relevant to the subject discussed in individual chapters at the time of design or construction. Today, if desired, conversions may be found easily on the internet. Rail gauge may be taken to be so-called 'Standard', 4ft 8½in (1435mm), except where stated otherwise.

The author has found the Web of value in assisting his researches, but to avoid clutter, with one exception (Chapter 22), no site addresses have been included herein, his feeling being that users wishing to pursue a line of interest themselves will have a good idea of which key words to enter into a search engine, while the main sources are identified within the relevant chapter. He has leaned heavily on the work of others, many whose names are not known to him and many whose are, and it would be unforgivable for him not to acknowledge the assistance provided over the years by friends, acquaintances and others unknown in countries around the world; here at home, but also in particular Argentina, Australia, France, Germany, South Africa and the United States. They have given generously of their time to seek out information, to provide the drawings and photographs which now fill numerous files in the author's collection, and demonstrate that the railway interest is one which is truly sans frontières. Last but certainly not least, thanks are due to Adam Harris at Camden for his advice and support, and to Andy Luckhurst for tackling the design task so well.

PART ONE

LOCOMOTIVES THAT WERE

CHAPTER ONE

1814 BRUNTON LOCOMOTIVE, UK
3ft 6in Gauge

Richard Trevithick's pioneer Penydarren locomotive of 1804 demonstrated conclusively that smooth wheel on smooth plate, or rail, could provide sufficient traction for practical operation, but at the same time revealed a problem that was to vex the early engineers in the field, namely that weight required caused the locomotive to fracture the brittle cast iron (or pot metal) tracks.

The first steam railway locomotives to see commercial use, of the Murray-Blenkinsop arrangement on the Middleton Railway in Leeds (from 1812), avoided the problem by gaining traction through a toothed wheel which engaged with a rack laid to one side of the running rails. This arrangement also found employment at the Kenton & Coxlodge, Tyneside, and Orrell, Wigan, collieries, while two further examples were constructed in Berlin (1816-1818). Other means of spreading weight but maintaining traction included taking chain drive from the locomotive to the leading axle of its tender, and by William Chapman's method, in which the locomotive hauled itself along by means of a chain laid between the rails. One was constructed by the Butterley Company in 1813 and delivered to Heaton Colliery, Newcastle, where it ran, it seems only intermittently, until May 1815.

The Butterley Company, of Ripley, Derbyshire, was founded in 1790, growing into a substantial coal and iron concern, and in the early 19th Century, amongst a variety of products, was a producer of stationary steam engines. In addition, it not only constructed

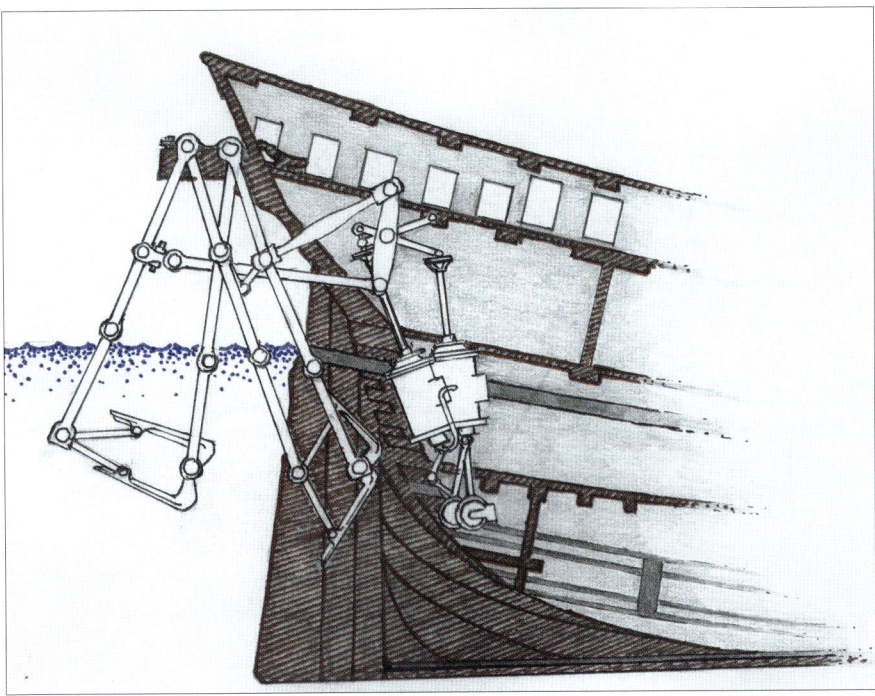

William Brunton was not the first to have the idea of employing legs and feet powered by steam as a means of propulsion. In 1776 the Marquis Claude François Dorothée de Jouffroy d'Abbans completed a 42ft long Newcomen engine steamboat so powered, which he called Palmipède ('web foot'). The accompanying drawing illustrates what is said to have been the arrangement of the mechanism, but it is unclear as to whether or not it represents the form in which the vessel was completed. It is said also to have been tried on the river Doubs during June and July of that year, without success. Seven years later, his second attempt, his Pyroscaphe (from the Greek 'fire boat'), fitted with paddles rotated through a double ratchet system, did on a single occasion sail a short distance under its own steam. In this country, in 1824, David Gordon completed a three-wheel steam carriage with a two-cylinder engine which drove feet by means of a six-throw crank system. His idea was that the feet would grip a rough surface without causing damage to the road. Four were built; they did work, but disappointed, and like Brunton's locomotives proved an evolutionary dead end.

---

the solitary Chapman locomotive, but two of the kind pictured here, to the patent of the Scot William Brunton (1777-1851), at the time employed by the company as an engineer. His Patent No.3700 of 22 May 1813 described 'machinery for drawing or propelling carriages on roads and railways, also vessels on water, by levers, acting alternately or conjointly.' (In total, between 1813 and 1842, he took out nine patents, although all but the first related to such products as fire-grates, furnaces and excavating machinery.) Two locomotives were built to his arrangement, both at his own expense, the first (1813) at a cost of £240, entered into the Butterley ledger as 'Horse made for Crich Railway.' Brunton described it as a steam powered 'Propeller', having a single-flue wrought iron boiler 5ft 6in long by 3ft diameter, fired when stationary, feeding steam to a single 6in by 4in cylinder. Weight in working order was 2¼ tons, boiler pressure 40 to 45 lb/in². The machine's small size is evident in the accompanying painting, and perhaps it is best described as having been a technology demonstrator. It is recorded as having attained a speed of 2½ mph up a 1 in 50 grade along the plateway connecting the Butterley quarries at Crich to Amber Wharf on the Cromford Canal.

Clearly it functioned acceptably, as in September 1814 Brunton had a second example constructed. Costing him £540, it was made to 4ft 0in gauge edge rail, and considerably enlarged, having two cylinders and weighing 5 tons. It was moved disassembled to John Douthwaite Nesham's Newbottle Colliery, where it was put together by the Butterley fitter Thomas Grice and set to work on the 6 mile line connecting his coal pits and staithes on the River Wear at Sunderland, along which it proved capable of propelling ten to twelve loaded wagons up a 1 in 36 gradient. After some months, it was decided to increase its capacity to twenty wagons, for which reason in the mid-summer of 1815 it was fitted with a new, enlarged boiler. Tragically, this led to the world's first railway disaster. On 31 July, the occasion being the initial test of the new boiler, Brunton's locomotive exploded in front of a group of colliery employees and curious bystanders, killing three immediately and injuring fifty more, some of whom later succumbed. The cause of the accident lay in over enthusiasm on the part of the driver, William Sharp, who it was stated 'overcharged' the boiler, which may not have been provided with a safety valve or fusible plug. It was not subsequently repaired.

The author's representation is conjectural, as there are no illustrations of either locomotive as completed, the only available information lying in Brunton's patent application, which simply outlines a single cylinder, boiler mounted on a four-wheel chassis, with the legs and feet attached at one end. There are old sketches which indicate also a chimney emerging from one end of the boiler and firedoor at the other, located beneath the cylinder and difficult to access between the operating legs; these are guesswork, although reasonable, as Brunton himself did state firing would be carried out when the locomotive was stationary. The geometry of the motion as drawn in the patent specification, and in later interpretations of it, would have resulted in damage to the piston rod (first pointed out by Loughnan Pendred to the Newcomen Society in 1922), and the author, guided by the late Leslie Charlton, has added the Y-shaped anchorage to the boiler endplate in order to provide a secure fixing for the two links attached to it, thus forming a parallel motion. Sadly, Brunton's patent locomotives have been treated unfairly, the butt of many jokes, as bearing in mind the state of knowledge and metallurgy of the time, they represent a considered approach to the problem of weight and rail fractures. It is worthy of record that the Newbottle example was one of the first handful of steam railway locomotives to see regular commercial service anywhere in the world. In the painting the Crich engine is seen propelling, undoubtedly its normal mode of operation.

The Butterley Company 1790-1830
Philip Riden, Derbyshire Record Society Vol. XVI 1990

The Crich Mineral Railways
'Dowie', Tramway Publications 1971

The Practical Dictionary of Mechanics Volume III
Mifflin, Boston, USA (19th Century, undated) (de Jouffroy)

A History of Railway Locomotives down to the end of the year 1831
C.F. Dendy Marshall, LPC 1953

The First Locomotive Engineers
L.G. Charlton, F. Graham 1974

CHAPTER TWO

1856 PENNSYLVANIA RAILROAD, USA
Baldwin 4-4-0 No.134 *Tiger*

For many years one of the most widely used steam locomotive wheel arrangements was the 4-4-0, in most parts of the world regarded as best adapted to passenger train haulage, though after the first decade of the 20th Century one that in general was employed on the less demanding duties. There were exceptions, as is always the case, Britain's Southern Railway three-cylinder Schools Class of 1930, for example, the forty members of which demonstrated consistently an ability to run fast and pull hard. In the United States, where the type originated, it started out as a load hauler, there being little demand for speed. The first was the brainchild of H.R. Campbell, chief engineer of the Philadelphia, Germantown & Norristown Railway, for which it was built in 1837 by Brooks of Philadelphia. In May of that year it demonstrated its ability to pull 450 tons at 15 mph on level track, but it was not representative of what was to come. It had inside cylinders and a short coupled wheelbase, while the over-rigid suspension led to a tendency to derail. More successful was Eastwick and Harrison's *Hercules* of the same year, which had flexible running gear and adapted itself more easily to the generally indifferent track of the time. It included a form of equalising lever, bringing with it the three-point suspension, which in partnership with a longer wheelbase and almost without exception outside cylinders, transformed the 4-4-0, or 'Eight Wheeler', into what was to become during the 19th Century the most popular locomotive type in the USA. Indeed, it would not be outrageous to claim that it was the 'American', as it was known, that built the infrastructure of the nation.

By 1855 there were about 6000 locomotives in the United States, a majority of which were the long wheelbase 4-4-0, as pictured here. As late as 1884 the arrangement accounted for 60% of new locomotives purchased by US railroads, yet within a decade this had reduced to 14%, and by the start of the 20th Century it was regarded as obsolete. The reason was

For American railway locomotives, the period 1850 to about 1865 was one of bright ornamentation. Corporate imagery was unknown, the often highly elaborate decoration reflecting the preferences both of the locomotive builders themselves and of proud footplatemen. This is understandable; the men were aristocrats, the new railways were a source of pride, the bringers of civilisation to remote lands and the symbol of the new age of industry. One can imagine the reassurance felt by the young woman at the sight of *Tiger* passing by her lonely farmstead. Primary colours appear to have been favoured, green and red in particular, while elaborate lining was commonplace, together with illustrated panels incorporating portraits of public figures, landscapes, wild birds and animals, even sometimes of factories. Chimneys, or stacks, might be red. In order to keep their charges looking smart, the footplatemen, most usually the fireman, would lavish on them metal polish, linseed and sperm whale oils. The accompanying painting is based on a beautiful coloured lithograph by Jonathan Ord and issued by the maker, Baldwin; the printer was L.N. Rosenthal of Philadelphia. While the details of the decoration may be taken as accurate, the colour rendition cannot be absolutely guaranteed. On the lithograph, though, the locomotive's tender is definitely pink. The dreadful slaughter and savagery of the divisive Civil War between 1861 and 1865, in which railways for the first time played a central rôle, undoubtedly was influential in dampening the enthusiasm for extravagant decoration, and thereafter locomotives were turned out in more sombre fashion. While often they continued to be lined-out elaborately, and beautifully polished, the bright colours had gone, replaced by black. Many years later, with the coming of the streamliner era, first with steam and shortly after with diesel and electric, bright colours reappeared, on locomotives and entire train sets, but they lacked the wonderful variety and individuality of the mid-19th Century, rather were they, by and large, the commissioned work of professional stylists. Today advertising agencies all around the world employ the slab sides of modern electric locomotives in particular for promotional displays; bright, and on occasion interesting, they are ephemeral, but a pale shadow of the exuberant hand-painted artistry of more than a century and a half ago.

Today brightly coloured locomotives and trains abound, but they are not a reflection of a builder, craftsman painter, or railwayman's pride in product or trade, rather a form of advertising speedily applied in vinyl and just as speedily removed. Sometimes, certainly, the product concerned is the train operator itself, or maker, as in this image of a new Class 800 bi-mode multiple unit at Edinburgh Waverley, its body decoration promoting the identity of its maker Hitachi. Alternatively, as on Edinburgh Trams No.266, the decoration forms a part of an advertising campaign by business, in this case the double-glazing and home improvement specialist C. R. Smith. All-over wraps have never held great appeal to the author, but this example he has to admit to being well executed and definitely eye-catching.

---

the considerable improvement made to the tracks it ran on, and also greatly increased train weights, but in its day it had met all the requirements of the railroads, handling passenger and freight working with equal facility. In 1872 the American Railway Master Mechanics Association, in its annual report, stated 'eight-wheel engines do the same work at much less cost,' referring to 2-6-0 and 2-8-0 locomotives as running 'much harder, with much more friction and wear of the track than a common eight-wheel engine.'

Between 1868 and 1910 the Pennsylvania Railroad acquired 1365 4-4-0s, eventually consisting of 56 classes and sub-classes, the largest of which was D16b of 1900-1908, totalling 262 examples. Remarkably, the final three PRR 4-4-0s, Class D16sb, were not withdrawn until 1950, latterly having worked the lightly laid tracks of the company's subsidiary Baltimore & Eastern Railroad. The locomotive depicted here, PRR No. 134 *Tiger*, of course had long departed the scene. Turned out by Baldwin of Philadelphia in 1856, it had been withdrawn in May 1875. As built, the cylinders were 15in by 24in and coupled wheels 66 inch diameter, but the former at some point were increased 1 inch in diameter and the latter reduced to 60 inch. Weights in working order were 59100 lb and later 62500 lb.

A History of the American Locomotive: Its Development; 1830-1880
J.H.White Jnr, Dover Publications NY 1979

Iron Horses American Locomotives 1829-1900
E.P. Alexander, W.W. Norton 1941

Pennsy Power III
A.F. Staufer, Staufer 1993

CHAPTER THREE

1858 EDINBURGH, PERTH & DUNDEE RAILWAY, UK
Bouch/Scott & Company *Carrier*

To those of us who live in Edinburgh and along the shores of the River Forth, the Forth Railway Bridge is simply there, in the background of our daily existence, and often it will take the reaction of a visitor, friend or stranger, to remind us just what a remarkable structure it is. Ceremonially opened on 4 March 1890 by a Prince of Wales eager to get out of the wind and in to lunch, its statistics tell the story – 1½ miles (2.53 kilometres) in length and 361 feet (110 metres) in height above the high water mark – and today carrying as many, if not more, trains than ever. The design of John Fowler and Benjamin Baker (knighted for their efforts), it dominates the river both physically and historically, but in so doing diverts our attention from another outstanding, earlier Victorian engineering achievement, though one now long gone. An inspired conception, only a short distance to the east, this was the Granton to Burntisland train ferry, which began regular service in February 1850. Despite the fact that two broad river estuaries had to be crossed, of Forth and Tay, the coming of the railway initially greatly reduced the travelling time between Edinburgh and Dundee from around two days to just 3½ hours. Its advance was piecemeal; from Edinburgh Scotland Street to Trinity in August 1842, and from there on to Granton in February 1846, taking advantage of the existing two mile passenger ferry crossing to Burntisland, although the tracks did not extend on to the middle pier at Granton until June the following year. All well and good, but there remained considerable inconvenience in that passengers and goods had to change

How sad that Thomas Bouch should be remembered, not for this innovative and highly successful invention, but for the disaster that befell his Tay Bridge. It opened to great acclaim on 1 June 1878, but collapsed in that terrible storm of 1879, not long after he had received a knighthood. The following year, a broken man, he died in Moffat, at a distance from both his lasting triumph and failure. It was a good thing that he did not live to see the construction of John Fowler and Benjamin Baker's great bridge over the Forth, the replacement for his proposal, a double suspension bridge at Inchgarvie, on which work had commenced, but was immediately abandoned following the disaster on the Tay.

Above: The grave of Sir Thomas Bouch in Edinburgh's Dean Cemetery, his career condensed into just two words, lasting achievements buried beneath the wreckage of his Tay Bridge, its collapse an event that left him broken in body and in spirit. Perhaps here, in this grand burial ground, among the great and the good, he found peace and acceptance.

1849 and 1881, essentially of the same layout, but progressively larger. Their arrangement may be seen from the accompanying painting, there being a separate engine for each paddle, freeing up space between. The ferries were *Leviathan* (1849) and *Robert Napier* (1850), both by R. Napier & Sons, Glasgow; *Carrier* (1858) by Scott & Co., Greenock; *Balbirnie* (1861) by S. & H. Morton, Leith; *Kinloch* (1865) by A. & J. Inglis of Glasgow and *Midlothian* (1881) by Ramage & Ferguson, Leith. The gross tonnage rose from the 399 of the first built to 920 of the last. The subject of the painting is *Carrier*, which was built for the Tay crossing; it is pictured here at Granton, although it did not see regular use on the Forth until the opening of the second Tay Bridge in 1887. It had an interesting career; sold to S. L. Mason of Edinburgh in 1881, three years later it passed to the Isle of Wight Marine Transit Company, then to the London, Brighton & South Coast Railway in 1887, before finally moving to Sweden, where it was broken up in 1893. The ferries passed their lives painted plain black with the exception of *Carrier*, which could be distinguished by its white paddle box facings. They were intended for goods traffic, avoiding double transshipment, saving time, money and lessening the chance of breakages. Passenger vehicles, and on rare occasions locomotives, were carried, when being transferred to or from the Burntisland repair shops. In 1867 90681 tons of goods and 1187 wagons of livestock crossed the Forth, while four passenger craft carried 92830 travellers. The average time spent from commencement of loading at one side of the river and finish of offloading at the other was 56 minutes. Use of the ferry by passengers was permitted if they had missed their proper connection, but they crossed exposed to the elements on the open deck, while the deceased could also make use of the service, their coffin secured in a covered van. Additionally, on a number of special occasions, passengers did cross seated in carriages. For example, on the opening of the new harbour at Tayport (Ferryport-on-Craig renamed), the invited guests were taken over in this manner, while on the night of 28 December 1879 the North British directors did likewise on the *Leviathan*, hurrying to the scene of the Tay Bridge disaster. In 1881, the same vessel, by then kept as a standby, was pressed into service to carry the Burntisland militia to a review in Holyrood Park, Edinburgh, but on returning struck Burntisland pier and sank in the shallow water. The militia disembarked through the mud, amused bystanders being entertained, not by the sound of the band, but by some choice language.

modes of transport up to four times, if their destination was Dundee. In Fife, the railway from Burntisland to Ferryport-on-Craig, on the south bank of the Tay, opened in May 1848. Construction of the different sections of line had been undertaken by independent companies, but all were absorbed by the North British Railway on 29 July 1862.

The ferry was a success from the start and formed the basis of the roll-on/roll-off vessel, unaltered to this day, except in detail (size and form of propulsion, for example). The breaks in journey were time consuming and costly, but Thomas Bouch, manager and engineer of the then Edinburgh & Northern Railway, observing operations, conceived the idea of what he called the 'floating railway' which he promoted vigorously to his Board. It had three main elements; an inclined pier, a 'flying bridge' to the vessel's deck (self adjusting ramp), and a flat deck with the rails inset. An inclined ramp at the side of the pier had two parallel sets of standard gauge tracks, upon which rested a moveable frame, 61ft in length, running on 24 wheels (six per rail), its movements up and down matching the rise and fall of the water (there is a difference in levels of approximately 20ft between low and high tides). At the outer end of the frame was a link span lifted and lowered by two hand-turned winches. The ferries themselves, referred to as 'Goods Boats', although a part of Bouch's conception, were designed by Thomas Grainger. Six were constructed between

The North British Railway
C. Hamilton Ellis, Ian Allan 1959

The North British Railway, A History
D. Ross, Stenlake Publishing 2014

Burntisland, Fife's Railway Port
P. Marshall, The Oakwood Press 2001

Steamers of the Forth
I. Brodie, David & Charles 1976

CHAPTER FOUR

1865 GREAT NORTHERN RAILWAY, UK
Sturrock 400 Class 0-6-0 (+ 0-6-0 Steam Tender)

The first steam-tender locomotives proper to see use almost certainly were seven designed by Claude Verpilleux (1798-1875), a French mine labourer who became over time a prominent engineer, manufacturer and inventor. His brother also appears to have played a part in the design, which was the subject of Patent No. 9069 of September 1842. To a gauge of 1448mm, with four cylinders 220mm by 750mm and of 0-4-0+0-4-0 wheel arrangement, they worked coal trains between St Etienne and Rive de Gier for about a decade from 1842 and were able to move 40 empty wagons upgrade. It was later proposed to convert them to compound expansion, employing the Verpilleux-Baldeyrou system, patented in 1857, but by then they were no longer in operation and so the alteration was not carried out. In Britain, the steam tender arrived in 1859, on four of Benjamin Connor's Caledonian Railway 2-4-0s, Nos.193-196, but almost immediately they were transferred to the next batch, Nos.197-200, which appeared from the company's St. Rollox works the following year. They were not well received and it was only a short time before the engine units were removed from the tenders. Others of the type, built by Neilson and Beyer Peacock were to have been equipped similarly, but the orders for these were cancelled prior to construction.

The most numerous fleet of steam tenders, and the longest serving, belonged to the Great Northern Railway, totalling 50; 20 built new and 30 modifications by Doncaster Works of older redundant conventional tenders. In use between 1863 and early in 1869, they did see extensive operation, but probably caused as many problems as they solved. Their proponent and instigator was the GNR Locomotive Engineer, Archibald Sturrock (1816-1909), who had arrived from the Great Western Railway in 1850 on the recommendation of I. K. Brunel. Sturrock's contribution to the financial well-being and reputation of the GNR was substantial, through the locomotives and carriages which he designed, but rather less so through his steam tenders. To his Patent No. 1135 of May 1863, they were intended not only to be of financial benefit to the GNR, but also to himself. Serious development of the tender began in the spring of that year, its purpose being to increase train loads and thus reduce the number of movements, with a positive effect on congestion and on the number of locomotives required. The patent envisaged two 12in by 17in cylinders, fed from the boiler through a copper steam pipe with five bends, approximately 23 ft in length, but sufficiently flexible as not to require compensating joints. There were three coupled axles, the cylinders, located between the frames, connected to the centre one. Exhaust steam passed to separate 15-tube condensers set in the base of the water tank, non-condensed steam exiting through two vertical pipes at the rear of the tender. The valve gear was Stephenson link.

An impression of one of the Verpilleux locomotives at work. Keeping all those pipe connections steam tight must have been quite a task.

The twenty new-build tenders were attached to new locomotives, Nos.400-419 by Kitson of Leeds and R. W. Hawthorn, delivered over 1865-1866. Other locomotives of the same class, numbered up to 469, were supplied in the same period by the aforementioned makers, also by Avonside, Neilson and Vulcan Foundry, 30 of which had unpowered tenders and 20 of which came without tenders. The second batch of Hawthorn engines, Nos. 461-469, was to have been delivered with steam tenders, but the order was cancelled. The steam-tender equipped engines could certainly move a heavy load, but the trains they hauled were inconveniently long, while they were heartily disliked by the enginemen. One reason is evident from the painting; when running in reverse the men's vision could be seriously impaired by steam escaping from the tender. In summer, they would be trapped between heat emanating from the locomotive firebox and from the tender, the motion work of which was prone to damage, reflected in unwanted time out of service and in maintenance costs. Sturrock's successor, Patrick Stirling, who took over in October 1866, saw little value in continuing. In his report on the subject he wrote that they permitted only a "trifling reduction in the number of trains," "that engines had to be stopped because their tenders were under repair," "firebox and boiler tubes were overstressed," "the enginemen disliked them," and "water was blown out of tender waste pipes uncondensed." However, tenders could be switched from one engine to another, and in this painting we see a Neilson-built example coupled to a new-build steam tender, differing from the older, modified kind in the greater height of the side panels. In December 1866 the company decided to cease heavy repairs of steam tenders, a decreasing number remaining in use for just over two years. The running gear was put up for sale at £45 a set, two of which the enterprising I. W. Boulton of Ashton-under-Lyne was able to turn into locomotives. The Manchester, Sheffield & Lincolnshire Railway for a short period from 1863 operated seven 0-6-0s paired with Sturrock steam tenders, but although further orders were mooted as late as 1866, they were never placed. In the same period, the Est (France) and Grand Central Belge each briefly operated two of the type. In 1869 Neilson supplied ten to the Cordoba & Belmez in Spain; built to Sturrock's patent, they differed in having cylinders and valve gear outside the frames. Much later, between 1915 and 1918, at its Spencer shops the Southern Railway in the USA modified six almost new Class Ms 2-8-2s, Nos.4535-4539 and 4576, equipping their tenders with engine units from obsolete 2-8-0s. In addition, No.4561 of the same class was provided with the engine unit of a 1889 Rogers 2-6-0, while one Class Ss 2-10-2, No.5046, received a new-build 2-6-2 arrangement with piston valves and Walschaerts valve gear. The Ms engines lost their 'boosters' in 1923 and No.5046 in 1926. Utilised over the heavy grades of the company's Asheville Division, they were considered reasonably successful, but in many respects also almost certainly something of an inconvenience.

Great Northern Locomotive History Vol.1 1847-66
N. Groves, RCTS 1966
Archibald Sturrock, Pioneer Locomotive Engineer
T. Vernon, Tempus Publishing 2007
Articulated Locomotives
L. Wiener, Constable 1930
Railways, The Pioneer Years
M. Fletcher / J. Taylor (Eds.), Studio Editions 1990

CHAPTER FIVE

1876 GRAZ KÖFLACHER BAHN, AUSTRIA
GKB Graz 2-2-0T (Inspection Car)

When the author first travelled the length of the Graz Köflacher Bahn in May 1965, it remained as it had been for a hundred years, a coal carrier operating second-hand steam locomotives, some of them centenarians still in everyday service. Opened in April 1860 under the title Voitsberger – Köflacher – Lankowitzer Steinkohlen Gewerkschaft, later GKB, in 1878 it was absorbed by the Südbahn, before in 1924 reverting to its previous ownership. During 1928 the giant Österreichisch Alpine Montangesellschaft took a majority shareholding in the GKB. Following the Anschluss of March 1938 the GKB rolling stock was taken over by the Deutsche Reichsbahn, but the locomotives retained their existing numbers and apparently their independence. In July 1945 it was returned to its pre-Anschluss status.

Today it functions largely as a passenger railway under the title GKBahn und Busbetrieb GmbH, operating new Stadler GTW 2/8 diesel units and also buses, the most important public transport provider in West Styria.

It was conceived as a carrier of the soft brown coal (lignite) mined around Köflach to the main line Südbahn connection at Graz, and along an additional line from Lieboch to Wies-Eibiswald opened in 1873. Even so, there was always a passenger service, largely operated after 1953 by Uerdingen diesel railbuses, but as late as 1965, in the morning and evening, on high days and holidays, it was augmented by trains of characteristic four-wheel carriages hauled by the last two 4-4-0 steam locomotives active in Europe. Former Südbahn Type 17c, purchased by the GKB in 1924. GKB 372 (pictured) and 415, they retained their original numbers. On the occasion of the author's visit, although in rather grubby external condition they were clearly in first class mechanical order, in steam at the company's Graz depot and ready for the late afternoon rush. Also present there, although probably no longer in use, was one of the outside-frame 0-6-0s so typical of old Austria, No.677, dating back to 1860. However, its sister of the same age, No.671, the author came across shunting at Lieboch. Watching this wonderful veteran, quietly, without fuss, moving coal wagons along the sidings, he quite ignored the fact he was being soaked to the skin in a downpour. Freight trains were hauled by another classic old-Austrian type, the Golsdorf two-cylinder compound 2-8-0, some of which retained the distinctive Kobel spark arrester chimney and Clench steam drier connecting the two domes (as on 56.3200 pictured here). Happily, No.671 was declared a National Monument in 2004 and is retained by the present day company in working order, while the 4-4-0 No.372 resides at the Strasshof railway museum near Wien. Its companion, No.415, is with the Brenner & Brenner organisation at St. Pölten.

Perhaps, though, the most interesting GKB steam locomotive of all, also certainly the least known, is the one pictured here. As may be seen, it was of decidedly diminutive dimensions (those known to the author were published in Imperial); there were two cylinders 2.75in by 4.75in (69.85mm by 120.65mm), while the boiler, which contained eight copper tubes, worked at 118 lb/in² (8.03 atm). The steam dome included a Ramsbottom safety valve, with in addition a brass-cased spring balance example atop the firebox. A common old-Austrian feature was the filler cup on the boiler. Completed at the company's Graz workshops in 1876, it may have been an apprentice exercise, and was intended for stationary operation, the cylinders connected to double-flanged wheels which could accommodate a drive belt for machinery. An eccentric on the axle drove the feed pump and a copper pipe leading to the base of the chimney formed the blower. The valve gear was Gooch. Shortly after completion, however, it was placed on a four-wheel chassis which had seats at each end able to accommodate eight persons in all, the four seated at the rear having the advantage of protection from the elements, in one direction at least. The drive was by belt from the double-flanged wheels on the engine to the rear axle of the carriage. It must have made a pretty picture skipping along at its maximum 20 mph (32.2 km/h), but it was to be for only a short period, as in 1878 the GKB was absorbed by the Südbahn. The latter had no time for such frivolities, and sold the little engine to a locksmith who set it up on a trestle and employed it to drive his machine tools. Sometime around the turn of the 19th-20th Century he changed over to electricity and sold the engine on to a Herr Hogler of the Südbahn, who purchased it on his own behalf as an addition to his 'private collection of steam engines and models.' Its subsequent history and ultimate fate is not known to the author.

Standing beyond is GKB No.13 *Sulm*, Österreichisch-Ungarische Staatseisenbahngesellschaft workshops, Wien (StEG) 1223/1872; it later passed to the Südbahn as Type 24 No.142, losing its name. In many ways it is typical of the era, with large smoke arrester, almost equally large dome with safety valve and filler cup atop the boiler; in others it is not. The coupled wheels are of smaller diameter than was usual for a 0-6-0 of the period, while the provision of inside frames caused the boiler to be set higher than normal in order that the firebox could sit astride the frames without reduction in size. This was an important consideration when soft brown coal was being burned.

The Locomotive
Issues of 15.11.1907 and 15.01.1909
Lokomotivbau in Alt-Österreich 1837-1918
K. Golsdorf, J.O. Slezak, Wien 1978
Author's notes and observations

The GKB yard at Graz on a dull and wet 31 May 1965; 4-4-0 372 (Floridsdorf, Wien, 768/1891) and 2-8-0 56.3200 (Wiener Neustadt 5390/1917) stand in steam and ready for their next duty. The latter sports a Clench steam drier and, unlike some of its stablemates, still retains the old Kobel spark arrester. Although it is not obvious, the low-pressure cylinder nearest camera is of much larger diameter than the high-pressure on the other side. Both locomotives were taken out of service three years later.

CHAPTER SIX

1894 McCARY LOGGING COMPANY
Filer & Stoller 0-6-0 (Oscillating Cylinder)

Oscillating cylinders have seen wide application, principally in stationary and marine engines, perhaps the first example of the latter being de Jouffroy's Palmipède of 1776 (Chapter 1), but are surely best known to those interested in railways for their use on live steam model locomotives. The earliest examples did not run on rails, for which reason they often had steerable wheels at the front, in order that they could move in a circle and not collide with furniture or walls. This was important, as if overturned they might leak burning paraffin. Aside from that, as they ran they would drip water, which is why they were often referred to as Piddlers, or Birmingham Dribblers. Famous early makers, beginning in the mid-19th Century, were the Stevens and Clyde Model Dockyards. Later oscillating cylinder models were of greater sophistication, running on rails, amongst the first of the kind being the O Gauge 2-2-0 tender locomotives by Johann Falk of Nürnberg, which came equipped with a safety valve. In this country, they possibly reached a commercial peak, at least in ready-made form, with the Model 234 introduced by Bowman Models of Dereham, Norfolk, in 1928. At first glance it appeared to be of 4-4-0 wheel arrangement, but in fact the drive was to the rear axle only. Those advocating oscillating cylinders for full-scale railway applications claimed they permitted more power to be transmitted to the crank pin than by any other means, while it was also argued that the fact there was no dead centre meant leverage was considerably enhanced. The great virtue of the type was its simplicity; the piston rods were coupled direct to the crank pin, thus obviating the need for connecting rods. Reversal was by means of a four-way rack through which the steam and exhaust chambers exchanged rôles. No valve gear was necessary, nor cut-off adjustment. In full-scale, however, the oscillating cylinder railway locomotive remained very rare. It was unsuited to anything other than limited, slow speed operation, although from time to time more ambitious proposals emerged. Patent No. 1857 of 1872, granted to William Dawes, outlined three different layouts utilising compound expansion with four cylinders located between the main frames. In one, the two high pressure cylinders were connected to the leading driven axle and low pressure to the rear, but the wheels were not coupled. The significant point is that the cylinders oscillated.

Filer & Stowell, of Cream City Iron Works, Milwaukee, Wisconsin, was set up in 1856 by Delos L. Filer, John M. Stowell joining as partner in 1883. The initial business of the company was providing machinery for sawmills, but it went on to produce stationary engines, including large simple and compound expansion examples of the Corliss type. During World War 2 it supplied engines for the mass produced Liberty cargo vessels, but perhaps it is best known for that familiar item of North American street furniture, the fire hydrant, which was made until the late 1930s. The company remains in business to this day, still supplying the logging industry. Less well known is that from the 1880s, probably into the early 20th Century, it was a regular producer of steam locomotives for the lumber companies, mainly located in the southern and south-eastern states. There were both standard and narrow gauge models, all tender types, of 0-4-0, 0-6-0 and 2-6-0 wheel arrangements, wood and coal burning. Logging railways often, though not universally, were rough and ready, regularly moved from one site to another, while conditions unsurprisingly could be primitive. The fact locomotives of this kind could operate only at slow speeds was not a limiting factor; of much greater interest to their owners was simplicity and low cost. The example illustrated here is a 0-6-0 tender locomotive, in itself a rare arrangement on logging railways, but a typical Filer & Stowell design. Crosshead, slidebar and cylinder pivoted around a cast trunnion, swinging up and down through an arc of 18 inches, the movement of the cylinder taking care of steam distribution. The trunnion contained two chambers, the centre having a single slotted port for each cylinder and the other having two ports serving the exhaust. While the arrangement dealt with the problem of high side forces at the crosshead where piston road and connecting rod join, it was difficult to prevent leakage, as steam passed through the cylinder pivots. A steam brake acted on the rear face of the leading coupled wheels and front of the middle pair. The tender paired with the example illustrated, turned out in 1894 for the S. F. McCary logging company, is a characteristic American type mounted on two two-axle bogies. What appears to be a steam dome is an open top cylindrical casing around the safety valves and whistle.

The other maker of oscillating cylinder locomotives, of which the author is aware, was Dewey Bros., Inc., of Goldsboro, North Carolina. Like Filer & Stowell, the firm started out as suppliers of equipment to the logging industry, but from about 1898 commenced production also of small locomotives particularly suited to the level ground and swamp country of the coastal South; they were made to gauges between 3ft and standard, adapted as required to wood or steel rail. Probably around twenty oscillating cylinder examples were completed up to about 1911; all were tank engines of 0-4-0 and 0-4-2 wheel arrangement. In 1913 the type was abandoned, production thereafter, until total cessation in 1925, being of locomotives with fixed cylinders and chain gear drive, plus a handful with rod drive. It has been stated that the Dewey oscillating cylinder engines did not enjoy great success as a result of insufficient oil reaching the trunnion, leading to excessive wear, the firm being unable to employ the more efficient method patented by Filer & Stowell. Another stated shortcoming was the high rate of water consumption, but one wonders how much of a problem this was in woodlands having many rivers, streams and ponds. The example pictured here is work's number 150 of July 1902, a 3ft gauge wood burner for the Mullen Lumber & Brick Company. It would appear no Filer & Stowell or Dewey Bros. oscillating cylinder locomotive has survived, although Dewey's No.110 of 1901, latterly with Wade & Morrison, contractors, was purchased by Henry Ford in 1926 at Weldon, North Carolina. Intended for his Museum, it subsequently disappeared.

A true giant of the O Gauge, Bowman's Model 234 oscillating cylinder live steam model, with tender, was 1ft 8in in length and 4½in rail to top of chimney (508mm and 114.3mm). Introduced in 1928, apparently of 4-4-0 wheel arrangement, it was actually 4-2-2-0 (or, simpler perhaps, German style 2'1A). A tank engine variant was also available, though sensibly both types were dispatched by the maker, not in cardboard but in stout wooden boxes.

Bulletin No. 112 April 1965
The Railway and Locomotive Historical Society (USA), Dewey Brothers Locomotives, M.J. Dunn III

Model Railroader May 1976
Filer & Stowell Logging Locomotives, A.J. Brewster

Model and Miniature Railways
J. Adams / P. B. Whitehouse, New English Library 1974 (in 45 parts; pages 862 to 864 in particular)

CHAPTER SEVEN

1906 NORTH EASTERN RAILWAY, UK
4CC Class 4-4-2 No. 731

The railway historian and artist Cuthbert Hamilton Ellis once wrote something to the effect that when it comes to railway locomotives – he was writing of steam – there were no rules in respect of appearance. This was ever so, and in truth applies universally; one man's triumphant Gothic cathedral is another's eyesore. When it comes to the steam railway locomotive, the author has always been attracted to the mechanically and visually unusual, and to the machine which shows sufficient of its working parts to make clear it has been designed to do a serious job. In other words, where form to a great extent follows function.

In Britain, and in parts of the world beneath its influence, from the time of *Rocket* in 1829 to about the first decade of the 20th Century, practicality, accessibility in particular, was not necessarily the designer's first priority. A plentiful supply of cheap labour and economic conditions which allowed locomotives to be out of service for extended periods being repaired and often meticulously repainted, were reflected in the high priority given to external appearance. Here, though, we have a locomotive, which while following this tradition, the author accepts as a real beauty. Simple in outline and most elegantly proportioned, it and one other were the work of the talented, even brilliant Walter Mackersie Smith, at the time of their construction in 1906 Chief Draughtsman of the North Eastern Railway. Normally, his function would have been to work up the ideas presented to him by his superior, Wilson Worsdell, the company's Chief Mechanical Engineer, but Worsdell, unlike many of his kind, was sufficiently confident as to delegate, and recognising Smith's talent, made sure he had the freedom and finance to pursue his ideas in respect of compound expansion. The latter's first effort had been to convert NER No.1619, an existing two-cylinder compound, to his own three-cylinder arrangement, with two low-pressure cylinders outside the frames and one high-pressure inside. A 4-4-0, again attractively proportioned, it proved a great success and despite being the only example of its kind ran from 1898 to 1931. It also formed the basis for the only large, long lived group of three-cylinder compound passenger locomotives to see service in Britain, the Midland Railway Johnson/Deeley 4-4-0s, 240 of which were constructed over the thirty years from 1902.

The first example of NER Class 4CC, No.730 (post-1923 LNER Class C8), emerged from the company's Gateshead Works in April 1906, followed one month later by its companion No.731 (pictured). The pros and cons of compound expansion as applied to railway locomotives continue to be discussed (see Chapter 35), but what is unarguable is that these two four-cylinder compounds not only looked good, they were also excellent performers. Indeed, in later years, many former NER enginemen recalled them as the finest express locomotives the company ever had. It has to be said that much of the motion was inaccessible, the valve gear being between the frames, but that was common practice in this country for many years and then would have caused no comment. Of 4-4-2 wheel arrangement, they had two high-pressure cylinders 14½ by 26in outside the frames and two low-pressure 22in by 26in inside, all connected to the leading axle. Controls were provided that allowed drivers to work them as simples, semi- or full-compounds, choosing which was most advantageous according to the demand placed on the locomotive. Coupled wheel diameter was 7ft 1¼in, boiler pressure initially 200 lb/in², later 225 lb/in² (both acquired new superheated boilers in 1915), grate area 29 ft² and maximum axle load 19t 12cwt. The three-axle tenders, whilst recognisably of NER outline, were in fact non-standard in detail; water capacity was 3800 gallons and coal 5 tons. The two locomotives externally differed little, but internally matters were otherwise, No.730 having Stephenson link motion actuating slide valves, No.731 Walschaerts with piston valves. Both were dual fitted, having Westinghouse air brake and vacuum.

Between 1906 and late in 1933, the pair were based at Gateshead, other than for a brief loan to the Botanic Gardens shed at Hull in spring 1931, but then moved from south to north of the River Tyne, to Heaton, from where they were taken out of service, No.730 in January 1935 and No.731 in December 1933. The latter had been sent for repair, but by then new Gresley Pacifics were available in numbers and as just two non-standard engines, without suitable work, their early withdrawal had become inevitable. The question might be asked, though; if they were so successful, why was the order for a further ten never fulfilled? The answer may be financial, as each cost £4661, which was almost £800 per engine more than Worsdell's own two-cylinder Atlantics, Class V, and it might have been felt the Directors of the company would be reluctant to authorise the expansion of the Smith type into a larger class. Smith had patented his arrangement, and it has been suggested alternatively the reason the type was not perpetuated was that his family demanded excessive royalties, but there does not appear to be any hard evidence this was the case. 1908 saw an interesting departure from routine, when the pair were loaned to the North British Railway for comparative trials with that company's own Atlantic, Class H (LNER C11), No.730 in June and No.731 in August. It proved an unhappy occasion for both. No.730 came to a stand on the ascent to Whitrope at the head of the 10.30am Edinburgh to Carlisle, in so doing slipping violently and causing the outside crank pins to fail, the consequence of which was it had to be taken off the train, while No.731 blew a gland on the right-hand high-pressure cylinder and also had to be removed. But between Newcastle and Edinburgh they were at home and worked between the two cities with sustained success for almost thirty years.

The location is the station at East Linton, on the east coast main line between Edinburgh and Berwick, and the occasion depicted might have been one of the very few, had the author been fortunate enough to be present, when the centre of his attention would not have been the stylish Atlantic. Rather it would have been the giant airship droning slowly through the skies to the west, an occurrence that would be as visually dramatic today as it was then. It can be dated to a day in June 1919, when the R34 was undergoing trials prior to successfully undertaking a 'first', a return flight over the North Atlantic, which of course included the first east to west crossing by an air craft. 643 ft (196 metres) nose to tail, it was powered by five 250hp 12-cylinder water cooled Sunbeam Maori petrol engines. Designed and assembled by William Beardmore & Co. Ltd. in an enormous specially constructed hangar at Inchinnan, Renfrewshire, it was quickly given the nickname 'Tiny', and took to the air there for the first time in December 1918. Early trials not unexpectedly threw up a number of problems, but there was no doubt as to its basic soundness, and on 28 May 1919 it flew east across Scotland to the Royal Naval Air Station at East Fortune, close to East Linton, where preparations were made for the trans-Atlantic attempt. Here R34 is returning to its base at the end of the day, we might suggest not long before its departure for New York in the early hours of 2 July. The crossing was not easy, the weather being unpredictable and at times violent, while the Sunbeam motors proved to be highly temperamental, but a safe landing was made at Roosevelt Field on Long Island four days later. The first non-stop flight over the Atlantic had been made just a fortnight earlier, albeit west to east from St. John's in Newfoundland, a heroic but one-way effort by two men in a modified twin-engine Vickers Vimy bomber which had ended nose-down in Derrygimla Moor, County Galway, Ireland. The R34 on the other hand had carried there and back thirty people, a stowaway (an aircraftsman who had been part of the crew, but removed against his will to free up weight for the inclusion of a US Navy officer as observer), and a kitten rescued from the streets of Renfrew by one of the ship's engineers. The return ended on an unfairly downbeat note when late on in the journey, against the expectations of the crew and of those waiting to greet them (including the press), the Air Ministry radioed an instruction that they were not to land at East Fortune, instead at Pulham in Norfolk, where they arrived to a muted reception. The R34, having suffered some damage on a training flight, was scrapped at Howden, Yorkshire, in January 1921, a sad fate for one of the best-designed and constructed large airships of the era.

Compound Locomotives
J.T. van Riemsdijk, Atlantic Transport Publishers 1994

Locomotives of the LNER Part 3A
Railway Travel & Correspondence Society 1979

Sir Vincent Raven and the North Eastern Railway
P. Grafton, The Oakwood Press 2005

Atlantic, The Well Beloved Engine
R.A.S. Hennessey, Tempus Publishing 2002

The Flight of the Titan, The Story of the R34
G. Rosie, Birlinn Limited 2010

CHAPTER EIGHT

1907 COMPAGNIE GÉNÉRALE des OMNIBUS, PARIS, FRANCE
Purrey 0-4-0T (Steam Tram Locomotive)

The steam tram, the 'Dummy' (USA), the 'Motor' (Australia), the 'self-propelled garden shed'; just a few of the terms applied to that homeliest of railway locomotives, the steam tram. Indeed, as has been remarked, when it stood there in the street, quietly panting, one almost felt moved to give its flanks a friendly pat. Those which ran along the streets by and large did so disguised inside a box-like body, in the hope they would not frighten horses and old ladies. There were many instances where as time passed the rules were relaxed, in particular in France and the Low Countries, their sphere of operation gradually spreading out into the countryside. Urban steam tram networks generally formed only a brief interregnum between horse-drawn operation and electrification. An exception was Sydney, the home of the steam tram system par excellence, in its day the largest in the world, and the true creator of the city's suburbs. Between 1879 and 1937, when the 5½ mile Kogarah to Sans Souci line was replaced by trolleybuses, the New South Wales Government Tramways operated over 100 locomotives, the great majority by Baldwin of Philadelphia. At the opening of the 20th Century, steam trams daily made 1200 journeys through the city, carrying behind them 70 million passengers annually. Known locally also as 'Juggernauts' and 'Manglers', they were regarded nonetheless with considerable affection. One isolated line operated separately by ferry interests became the last in the Sydney area to use steam; connecting Redbank Wharf with Parramatta, it ceased operation in March 1943. Unusually, it had carried a substantial goods traffic as well as passengers. The Sydney steam tram network surely was one of the most remarkable urban and suburban transportation systems to be found anywhere in the world.

The chief object of our attention here, though, is the tramways of Paris, the first city in the world to operate a form of public transport service. It commenced operation in 1662 under a concession authorised by the King and utilising enclosed carriages, a flat fare of 5 sols being charged, but it was not open to all, accepting only the 'bourgeois and persons of merit' - one can picture some lively exchanges at stopping places. Limiting its patronage in such a way proved disastrous and failure was swift, with the result that it was almost two hundred years before horse-drawn omnibuses were seen once again on the city streets. The first rails were laid on Paris streets in 1853, a limited service beginning two years later, but real expansion did not take place until after 1873. Steam had arrived in 1868, when a service began between Le Raincy and Montfermeil, employing locomotives to the Larmanjat centre guide rail system, but it proved short-lived, as did a service not involving rails. Passengers were carried in trailers hauled by a Lotz of Nantes steam tractor named *La France* between Champigny and the junction of the boulevards Voltaire and Richard-Lenoir. A second Larmanjat section at Trocadéro opened in 1872, but came and went equally quickly. After 1873 the pace quickened, with the result that by the commencement of the 20th Century, there were eleven different companies in operation, with little co-ordination between them, while the largest, Compagnie Générale des Omnibus (CGO) by 1910 was running eight routes with horse haulage, ten with steam, nine with compressed air and two with battery-electric, without doubt an engineering department nightmare. In addition, outside the city walls the Versailles route was equipped with overhead wire, such a provision within the walls being forbidden.

The first CGO battery car, a three-axle double-decker ('l'impériale', as this arrangement was known), was tested over the winter of 1893-1894, but the trial came to an abrupt end one day when the middle axle fractured while the tram was crossing the Place de la République. The principal had been established, however, and the CGO eventually owned a total of 85 two-axle battery cars, supplied by Fives-Lille and Société Alscacienne de Constructions Mécaniques. They were numbered 501 to 585; 586, by Fives-Lille, was shown at the 1900 Paris Exposition, but never entered service. The compressed air car introduced by L. Mekavski, concessionnaire of the Nantes tramways, also was successfully employed by the CGO. Most examples were single-ended double-deck trams, running on a two-axle chassis, but early in 1895 a batch of mechanically similar locomotives began operation. Two cylinders drove on the leading of three axles, the valve gear being Walschaerts. Length was 6550mm, width 2120mm and height 4700mm; weight in working order 18 tonnes. They were bi-directional with an open fronted driving position at either end. There were two reservoirs mounted transversely beneath the floor, one with a 300 litre capacity and the other, as standby, holding 175 litres; charged pressure was 12atm. A facility on the Avenue de la Reine generated compressed air, which was fed to four recharging stations. In all, the CGO operated 23 of these locomotives, but when they were taken out of service in July 1907, no longer up to the job, that was not to be quite the end of the story, as 12 were sent to the works of Valentin Purrey at Bordeaux-Bègles for conversion to his system. This was already familiar to the CGO, it having operated a total of 36 single-deck railcars and 50 double. These were single-ended, coke fired, with a boiler of Purrey's design, reliable, quiet runners and more powerful than the Serpollet boilered type. The company operated 60 of the latter in double-deck form between 1900 and 1913, although they suffered at least one spectacular boiler explosion. Purrey, in converting the Mekarski locomotives, whilst retaining the existing cylinders and valve gear, removed the centre axle; the external dimensions also were unaltered, but weight in working order was reduced to 12 tonnes.

There are preserved steam trams to be found around the world, but what better example to use as illustration than NSWGT No.103A, Baldwin 11676/1891. Withdrawn in 1937 on closure of the Kogarah line it passed initially to Sydney Ferries Ltd as 103, in 1943 to the Colonial Sugar Co Ltd, Rhodes, NSW, later to Commonwealth Engineering Ltd, Clyde, NSW, then on withdrawal in 1953 to the Steam Tram & Railway Preservation Society, Parramatta Park, where the body work was destroyed in an arson attack in June 1993. It was restored to operational condition as 103A over 2000-2001 for STRPS at its present home the Valley Heights Locomotive Depot Heritage Museum (easily reached by rail from Sydney). Here it is seen in operation at Valley Heights on 14 November 2010, accompanied by a B Class trailer (former C2). Double-deck versions could be particularly draughty and at one time conductors, on request, would provide ladies with 'modesty laces' to secure their skirts.

They were numbered in the series 1 to 12. The accompanying painting shows one of these engines, its square section chimney rendering it visually highly distinctive, standing at the Louvre on a quiet afternoon, perhaps shortly before the end of steam operation over the route on 1 October 1913, with two trailers, the leading one an electric tram which would be in charge beyond Porte de Saint-Cloude.

Les Tramways Parisiens
J. Robert, self published, 3rd Ed. 1992

The Continental Steam Tram
G.E. Baddeley, Light Rail Transit Association 1982

New South Wales Tramcar Handbook 1861-1961 Part 2
N. Chinn/K. McCarthy, South Pacific Electric Railway Co-operative Society 1976

Further reading: the author strongly recommends to any reader interested in Sydney's remarkable steam tramway system:

Juggernaut! A Story of Sydney in the Wild Days of the Steam Trams
D. Burke, Kangaroo Press 1997

CHAPTER NINE

1907 WOLGAN VALLEY RAILWAY, AUSTRALIA
Vale & Company 2-2-0T (Steam Railbus)

Australia had a walk-on part in the previous chapter; in this it stands centre stage, as what must have been one of the most spectacular industrial railways to be found anywhere. Hidden in the inaccessible rocky depths of the Blue Mountains and connected to the Great Western Railway's Sydney to Lithgow main line (as this part of the New South Wales Government Railways then was generally known) at Newnes Junction, the Wolgan Valley Railway followed a northerly course for 32 miles to the Commonwealth Oil Corporation's works at Newnes. The line abounded in severe curves and gradients; there was a gentle rise to its summit of 3960ft six miles from the junction, after which it dropped at 1 in 50 for another six, then ran roughly level as far as No.1 Tunnel, from which a descent at 1 in 25 took it through No.2 Tunnel to Constance, three miles short of Newnes. It will be understood that the gradients were against loaded trains carrying the oil products. The Commonwealth Oil Company (COC), London based, was set up to exploit shale-oil reserves in the remote Wolgan Valley, the plant and supporting township named after the managing director Sir George Newnes. In many respects, this was a surprising development, as by the end of the 19th Century the long established New South Wales shale-oil industry and the kerosene it produced was in decline, in particular superseded by the American product derived from petroleum. However, a world-wide boom in oil, and favourable geological reports which suggested a yield of 90 gallons of crude oil to 1 ton of raw shale, led to the decision to invest in the Wolgan Valley works. To be found also were seams yielding excellent coking coal. It was estimated that 600 to 1000 tons of products would be taken daily up to Newnes Junction, to the considerable benefit of the Government lines. As too often was the case with such undertakings, the expectations of promoters and investors were never to be realised. The COC receiver and manager in 1917, W. H. Fletcher, blamed the unions for their repeated strike action, claiming that shale production was only 86 tons per day and that as a result the cost of working Newnes was 80% higher than any other oil producing area in the world (the author is unable to suggest how blame should be apportioned, though it would appear that even without labour difficulties the operation would have been scarcely viable). In August 1927 the COC finally gave up and advertised all the machinery for sale, rolling stock in fit condition being moved to Newnes Junction for disposal, of which the oil tank wagons went to the Clyde refinery, Sydney, for further use. There were later attempts to revive the operation, 3000 gallons of crude oil being produced daily by the end of 1931 under the auspices of the Shale Oil Development Committee, yet four months after, work had ceased again. Final, formal closure came towards the end of 1937, when the recently formed National Oil Company set up new works nearby in the Capertree Valley. A pipeline was laid along the route of the railway and oil tank wagons continued to be loaded at Newnes junction, but the tracks were lifted and it is understood were shipped to North Africa during World War 2.

Mainline motive power was provided by four three-cylinder, three-truck Shay geared locomotives from the Lima Machine Works of Lima, Ohio, a specialised design highly suited to the rough and ready trackage of the US lumber industry. These were; No.1 *Constance* (1778 of October 1906), name on driver's side only; No.2 (1994 of September 1907); No.3 (2100 of July 1908); No.4 (2270 of December 1909). The first three weighed 70 tons, had 12in by 15in cylinders and tractive effort 29800 lb, while No.4 weighed 90 tons, had 14½in by 15in cylinders and tractive effort 40400 lb. What makes this quartet particularly interesting is that they were the only examples of the type to have side buffers and three link couplings; they were also vacuum fitted. No.4 was a powerful beast and did most of the main line work in later years, although had the habit of spreading the track – it would not derail, but wagons behind it would. No.1 was dismantled about 1918 and its boiler employed for stationary duty; Nos. 2 and 3 were still standing derelict in 1940, more or less complete, and were not cut up until 1956. When No.4 was finally scrapped is unrecorded, but it was still present, partially dismantled, in 1953. Initially, shunting within the works was carried out by a Kerr Stuart 0-6-0T (780/1908), which about 1912 went to Lithgow Ironworks, surviving in colliery service until 1954. The isolated location and lack of alternatives meant it was necessary for the COC to provide a passenger service to and from Newnes Junction. There were two bogie coaches, one reserved for special occasions, the other a 2nd Class 48 seater which was regularly used, hauled by one of the Shays. In 1911 a 10 seat 18hp four-wheel petrol railcar was purchased for the line; intended for mail and parcels traffic, in later years it saw considerable use in passenger service. Capable of reaching 40mph, from July 1924 its regular work was a return trip the length of the line each Friday. Prior to its arrival the COC in June 1907 had purchased a double-deck Clarkson steam road bus from the NSW Government Tramways in Sydney. In the early 20th century, Clarkson, of Chelmsford, Essex, supplied these vehicles to a number of UK concerns, including the GWR/LSWR joint operation around Weymouth, and to the National Steam Car Company in London. In 1905-1906 the firm also supplied four chassis and engine units to Sydney, where Angus & Son of Newtown added the bodies, two single and two double deck. The latter vehicles were numbered 3M and 4M, carrying 16 lower and 18 upper deck passengers, plus 2 beside the driver. Housed at the Newtown tram depot, they ran between Enmore and Wardell Road, but only from late April to late May 1906. They had two sets of two-cylinder 40hp engines and a kerosene fired semi-flash boiler working at 250 lb/in^2: length over body 20ft, chain drive to rear wheels. Both were written off the books by June 1907,

A smaller Shay than those on the Wolgan Valley, having two trucks only and 8in by 12in cylinders, Lima 618 of 1900 nonetheless in appearance was absolutely characteristic of the type. The only Shay ever to be seen in Britain, it was delivered to Alfred Hickman & Sons Ltd, and for something over a decade it worked at the Springvale Furnaces, Bilston, alongside a group of the simple, outside-cylinder 0-4-0 saddle tanks so common in British industry. The only known photograph suggests it carried neither buffing nor ordinary draw gear, and perhaps a simple rigid distance bar was employed, keeping it at a safe distance from tubs of molten slag, a duty for which the even torque of the Shay would have made it ideal.

No. 3M being sold to COC and converted to rail operation by Henry Vale & Son of Auburn, the work, apart from the obvious fitting of flanged wheels, including the removal of the top deck. The two tall narrow section hollow columns either side of the driver carried away the exhaust gases, a change from the original arrangement in which they exited via horizontal flues either side, beneath the driver's feet. Here we see it in Penrose Gorge, broken down, with Shay No.1 coming to the rescue, just emerging from No.2 Tunnel (known as Glow Worm). The author could not resist the temptation to paint such a scene, but whether or not it reflects reality is impossible to say. How much running, if any, the modified bus did on the Wolgan Valley Railway is unknown, although it seems certain it never entered regular service. Beyond doubt the conversion was carried out – No.3M was photographed in rail mode at Vale's works – but after that, who knows? Perhaps inspecting it prior to delivery the COC's managers said to themselves, "On second thoughts….."

Shays In The Valley, A History of the Wolgan Valley Railway
G. Hicks/D. O'Brien, NSW Transport Museum 1999

The Shale Railways of NSW
G.H. Eardley/E.M. Stephens, Australian Railway Historical Society 2000

New South Wales Tramcar Handbook 1861-1961
N. Chinn/K. McCarthy, South Pacific Electric Railway Co-operative Society 1976 (Clarkson steam bus)

CHAPTER TEN

1910 ÉTAT BELGE, BELGIUM
Type 36 2-10-0 No. 4405

André Chapelon, in his monumental work on steam locomotives, discussing the 2-10-0 wheel arrangement, mentions the Austrian Golsdorf compounds of 1906 and French Paris-Orléans 6000 Series of 1909, but omits the Belgian Type 36 introduced in 1910, surprisingly, as at the time it was the heaviest and most powerful freight locomotive in Europe. However, George Carpenter, who translated the book into English, in his addendum, does include the type, noting that on test one of the engines hauled 443 tonnes up a 2.5% grade at 21 km/h, around curves of 600 to 800 metres. A speed of 60 km/h was maintained with 1090 tonnes over almost level track. Prior to the coming of the Type 36, the heaviest freight duties were largely in the care of a series of inside-cylinder 0-6-0s which would not have looked out of place on the Caledonian Railway in Scotland; totalling 809 examples, 502 of which employed saturated steam (Type 32) and the remainder superheated (Type 32S). From thirteen Belgian makers, they belonged to the Période McIntosh, the years 1898 to 1914 during which many different locomotives, of 0-6-0, 4-4-0, 4-6-0 and 4-4-2T arrangement entered service, all directly influenced by the work of the Scottish engineer. The Type 36, therefore, was of a different order, although there was a charming reminder of the Scottish influence in the presence on these large, modern engines of prominent smokebox wing plates. The so-called Flamme era, which from 1905 until the outbreak of war in 1914 overlapped the McIntosh, saw the introduction of much larger locomotives, the best known of which are the 58 examples of Type 10 4-6-2, notable in having all four simple expansion cylinders in line well ahead of the smokebox and at their time of introduction in 1910-1912 the most powerful passenger locomotives in Europe. The genesis of the Type 36, though, perhaps lay in an unfulfilled 1908 proposal by the builder La Meuse for a 2-10-0 having 1450mm coupled wheels and a parallel boiler with narrow Belpaire firebox. A total of 134 Type 36 were constructed from 1910, and as was common in Belgium, but surely not cost effective, by no fewer than fifteen different firms, three of whom completed only one example, while the maximum number from one workshop was 20 (Gross Forges et Usines de La Hestre). The external appearance was similar to the Type 10 Pacific, in that the first three boiler rings were parallel, while the fourth tapered steeply upward to meet the large round-top firebox, which had a grate area of 5.1m². The front end layout differed, as the four 500mm by 660mm cylinders were placed in line beneath the smokebox, the outer pair driving on the centre coupled axle and the inner on the second. Valve gear was Walschaerts, laid out in a most unusual and one might suggest unnecessarily complicated manner. As with the Type 10, the valves of the inside cylinders were actuated from the outside pair by rocking shafts which extended in front of them. However, as may be seen in the painting, the drive to the valves of the outside cylinders was in part outside and in part between the main frames. The union link, combination lever, radius rod and expansion link were outside, but the usual provision of return crank and return crank rod (connecting the driven coupled wheel and expansion link) were omitted, being replaced between the frames by an eccentric on the second coupled axle actuating the expansion link from the inside via a rocking shaft. As a result the locomotive had the odd appearance of running with some of its motion work missing. On the other hand, no serious problems appear to have arisen, the type performing well from the start, though when in 1922-1923 seventeen new examples were constructed, the common disposition of Walschaerts was applied, alteration of earlier engines having commenced two years previously. Coupled wheel diameter was 1450mm, on a total engine wheelbase of 10115mm, flexibility being provided by knuckle joints in the coupling rods on the second, third and fourth axles, while the fifth was allowed 29mm movement to either side. At the front end the leading carrying and coupled axles were mounted in a Flamme 'bogie-Bissel.'

During World War 1 the activities of the 129 members of Type 36 then active were seriously disrupted. A number of the class were moved under German control to East Prussia and later the Ukraine, but 102 were successfully evacuated to France, where, because of their high axle loading, they saw only limited use. On 28 August 1916, under an agreement signed by the Belgian government exiled in Le Havre, 80 Type 36 were sold to Russia, including 24 examples which the Paris-Orléans had been operating since the previous September. Exactly how many reached St Catherine's Bay (later Murmansk) is not clear, as a small number, said to be seven, were lost at sea, while probably around 40 were never shipped. Of those that did arrive, not all were altered to the Russian 1524mm gauge; those that were worked in the Crimea. Although as early as 1928 only 12 remained active, they enjoyed a long life, working between Sebastopol and Simferopol, the last survivor not being withdrawn until 1953. Over time some at least were modified to render them better suited to local operating conditions, which dramatically altered their appearance. While the original short chimney was retained, a much taller dome was attached to the boiler and cab roof considerably heightened. The firebox carried on top two large air reservoirs and, characteristically Russian, hand rails were added along the edge of the running plate between cab and front buffer beam. In Belgium, by 1923, the number in service totalled 93, including 17 newly constructed. After 1925 they were successfully redraughted in the same manner as Type 10 had been, with double blastpipes and increased superheat. In July 1926, the SNCB was created, following which in 1931 the class was renumbered as 3600 to 3692, then, in January 1946 as 36.001 to 36.093, the last being the former 3600. Although the final Type 36 in Belgium ceased running in 1947, a large number of stored war damaged examples, never repaired, survived for at least two more years. The author was not fortunate enough to see one of these handsome machines, but came to be a great admirer of them, especially in their final form with that distinctive Belgian double chimney, capuchon to the fore. In particular this was through the medium of some fine images captured by C.R.L. Coles during the final weeks of peace in August 1939. And No.4405 (later 3605 and 36.005), pictured here? The first to be delivered

Another locomotive of Belgian design and construction which featured a part inside, part outside arrangement of Walschaerts valve gear was the group of light 1676mm gauge 2-6-0s delivered to Spain's Central of Aragón railway by Couillet of Marcinelle in 1892, numbers 21 to 30, later RENFE 130 2091 to 130 2100. Here, the eccentric rod, and this time the expansion link also, sit between the frames, with radius rod, combination lever and union link again outside (just discernible in the photograph). 130 2100, by then a veteran of 72 years, but smartly kept and in good condition, stands in steam at Valencia-Alameda, 19 April 1964.

to the État Belge, it was built by Forges, Usines et Fonderies de Haine-Saint-Pierre and specially prepared for the 1910 Éxposition de Bruxelles in an extraordinary livery of canary yellow, with bright carmine frames, wheels and bufferbeams. The boiler bands were picked out in red, while cab and tender sides were edged in brown. In reality HSP works number 715, for the purposes of the Exposition it was displayed, toute pimpante, as number 1000. Behind No.4405 stands a McIntosh era 4-6-0 (Type 35), the common feature being their Scottish smokebox wingplates.

Vapeur en Belgique Volumes I and II
P. Dambly, Blanchart & Cie 1989 and 1994
Russian Locomotives Volume 2
1905-1924, I. Nurminen / F.M. Page, self published 1992

CHAPTER ELEVEN

1910 REID-RAMSAY, UK

Reid-Ramsay 2'B+2'B (Steam Turbine Electric)

The pioneer of the steam turbine railway locomotive was an Italian, Professore Antonio (or Guiseppe) Belluzzo. In 1905 he completed his first prototype turbine, then two years later, in a piece of remarkably innovative thinking, had adapted to his specifications what has been described as a '0-6-0T built in 1876'. The centre axle was removed, the four remaining wheels acquiring a housing mounted against their outer faces, in which was contained a turbine consisting of two steam chambers and separate nozzles for forward and reverse; drive to the axles was through gearing. The original 10atm boiler was retained. There was no condenser, but the little prototype proved sufficiently successful to be retained as a works shunter for over a decade. The idea of the non-condensing steam turbine locomotive continued to be pursued over the years, without real success, except perhaps in Britain as applied to the LMS Stanier Pacific No. 6202, which though requiring careful maintenance, ran well, and in Sweden the three Ljungström 2-8-0s of the TGOJ, which from 1931 reliably moved ore from Grängesberg to Oxelösund until rendered redundant by the electrification of the route in 1953 (all three remain in existence). Professore Belluzzo was aware, however, as were other engineers who followed, that for best efficiency to be achieved, the steam turbine locomotive required a condenser. To the same end, the turbine requires to be run at consistently high outputs over extended periods, a fact which makes it very difficult to adapt successfully to rail operation, where power requirements are highly variable. The only successful long-term application has been of the gas turbine, where it was employed hauling heavy loads over considerable distances on the Union Pacific Railroad in the US between 1952 and 1969. Nonetheless, the form continues to interest railway administrations; as recently as December 2008 a 300 tonne prototype running on liquified natural gas was turned out by Russia's Voronezh workshops and one can envisage a useful application in the haulage of freight trains over the vast empty spaces between Asia and Europe. Despite the fact there were no such opportunities available in the British Isles, the steam turbine locomotive was essayed from time to time, with and without condenser, with electric or mechanical transmission, although its promoters may well have had export opportunities in mind.

The first to see daylight was the example illustrated here, a joint effort by the Hyde Park, Glasgow, works of the still youthful North British Locomotive Company and new-born Ramsay Condensing Locomotive Company. The two personalities leading the project were Hugh Reid (his father James had been sole proprietor of Neilson, Reid & Company, one of the constituents of NBL) and D. J. McNab Ramsay. Reid had first revealed the existence of the project in an October 1909 presidential address to the Glasgow University Engineering Society, the locomotive emerging from the Hyde Park erecting shops the following year under works number 19266. As may be seen it had a fully enclosed superstructure resting on a long rigid frame carried by two outside-frame pivoting trucks, in each of which were two adjacent powered axles and, in an attached inside-frame bogie, two unpowered. The locomotive was uni-directional and other than for short-distance and shunting movements was run condenser first (the chimney, therefore, was at the rear), both trucks being arranged with the unpowered axles leading, best described as 2'B+2'B, or in Whyte parlance, 4-4-0+4-4-0. There were four DC series wound traction motors with armatures on the four driven axles, current at 600V being supplied via a generator driven by an impulse turbine running at 3000 rpm. The powered wheels were of 4ft diameter. A conventional superheated locomotive type boiler working at 180 lb/in² was fitted, with fan induced exhaust. Optimistically numbered 1, it was titled ELECTRO-TURBO-LOCO in shaded block letters on the condenser casings, against a dark and unlined overall finish, suggested here to have been black. Some trial running was undertaken in the locality of Springburn, on both Caledonian and North British Railway metals, of which nothing appears to have been recorded, and the locomotive quickly retired into obscurity behind the walls of Hyde Park.

Fortunately, as things turned out, it was not dead, only sleeping, for with the Great War ended, Reid and NBL took up with enthusiasm a proposal brought to them by James MacLeod for adapting the geared steam turbine to drive a locomotive, greatly assisted by having this suitable candidate for conversion immediately to hand. To that end, in 1921 Reid (by now Sir Hugh) and MacLeod took out joint patents. The stored Electro-Turbo-Loco was dusted off and converted. The frames and boiler were renovated, while the two trucks were also re-used, but now with the unpowered axles at the outer ends, the notation becoming 2'B+B2', or 4-4-0+0-4-4. Mechanical transmission replaced electrical, the drive being via shafts through double reduction spur and bevel gearing, with a final flexible quill connection. There were two turbines, which appear to have been assembled in-house, working in series, the high and low pressure units and gearboxes being mounted at the inner end of each truck. Together the two turbines were expected to develop 1000hp at at 8000rpm, or about 950hp at the rail, the locomotive being intended to haul 225 tons at 60mph. These power units were enclosed in an oil tight casing and oil at a pressure of 20lb/in² was circulated continuously to all bearings and rotating parts. Although it still carried an enclosed bodywork, the appearance was considerably changed, the condenser arrangements at the front being altered, while the cab was shortened, with two arched windows either side of a central door. Now works number 23141 and described as the Reid-MacLeod Locomotive, as it had been in its original incarnation it was uni-directional, running condenser leading. Again, how it was painted is not known, but from what can be made out of the lining details, and darkish overall finish, it may have been the final North British Railway dark bronze green. What may be said for certain is that the paint had a mirror-like sheen, the reason being that shortly after emerging from the erecting shop in 1924, it was dispatched south for display at the famous Wembley Exhibition. A second public showing was intended the following year, in the procession at the Stockton & Darlington Railway centenary, for which purpose it was allotted position number 31. Sadly, but unsurprisingly, it did not appear. Testing did not go well. The LNER gave permission for trials to take place on the Glasgow to Edinburgh main line, wisely restricted to Sundays. The first outing did not occur until March 1926, and had to be abandoned at Greenhill (west of Falkirk), it is believed on the outward run, following problems with the circulating pumps. After a gap of more than twelve months, in April 1927, a second attempt was made. No. 23141 on that occasion reached Edinburgh Waverley with two carriages in tow, ran light-engine back to Haymarket for turning on the Gorgie triangle, then returned west with its lightweight load. Unfortunately, disaster struck; somewhere along the way there was a major turbine failure and that was that, it never ran again. The second illustration shows it on its way back to Glasgow on that final outing, obviously struggling. The location is Hallglen, between Polmont and Falkirk High, with one of the author's favourite childhood haunts, the Union Canal, at right. The canal remains, but the land beyond the railway is now built over with housing, while straddling the tracks are the masts of electrification.

Angturbinlok
B. Fornsberg, Svenska Järnvägsklubben 2001

Lokomotivbau und Dampftechnik
W. Stoffels, Pawlak 1991

Locomotives of the LNER
Part 10A, RCTS 1988

The Concise Encyclopaedia of World Railway Locomotives
P. Ransome-Wallis (ed.) Hutchinson 1959

CHAPTER TWELVE

P1 Class 1916 ERIE RAILROAD, USA
USA 2-8-8-8-2 No. 2603 (Henderson Triplex)

Emblematic of the steam railway locomotive age was the specialised banker, or pusher, a breed which has almost become extinct. Today, more commonly, because diesel and electric locomotives can operate in multiple but still require only one crew, additional power is either added at the head of the train, or is cut in, remotely controlled, at about the mid-point, running as such throughout the entire journey. But to those old enough to remember, the sight and sound of the steam banker hard at work would leave a memory to be savoured long after the event. In Britain, banking more often than not was undertaken by suitable goods and tank locomotives, the only concession to the duty perhaps a reinforced front buffer beam, specialised designs being few. In this connection one recalls the unique six-cylinder Beyer-Garratt introduced in 1925, LNER Class U1, which with a tractive effort of 72940 lb at the time was by far the most powerful locomotive in the country. Its function was to bank coal trains up 3.5 miles of 1 in 40 between Wentworth Junction and West Silkstone Junction in Yorkshire. Its 56.5 ft² grate was not stoker equipped and a demanding task for the single fireman carried but nonetheless it remained on the same job until moved south to the more famous Lickey Incline in 1949. It did little work there, and despite conversion to oil firing in 1952 was taken out of service in December 1955. The Lickey Incline, just over two miles rising at 1 in 37.7 towards Birmingham, lies on the main line from south-west England and has always carried a heavy traffic. Although initially Norris 4-2-0s had been imported specifically for use as bankers, followed by two specially designed tank engines, for many years the Midland Railway employed its standard goods tanks, singly, or in groups, dependent upon the weight of the train to be assisted. In 1903, a report dated 26 November recommended that 'specially designed engines should be provided for banking, not only for safer working of boilers, but also for efficiency.' The result was to become one of the best-known steam locomotives in Britain, the four-cylinder 0-10-0 No.2290 (later LMS 22290 and BR 58100). Authorised on 13 May 1914, its construction was delayed by World War 1, and it did not emerge until the very end of 1919. Operating within its design profile, that is, for short periods at high power outputs, it was popular and successful, but when in July 1924 it took the former L&YR dynamometer car and loaded coal train up the Midland main line (by then LMS) from Wellingborough to Cricklewood, London, it was unable to maintain steam pressure. It returned to the Lickey and worked until May 1956, when, worn out, it was withdrawn, although not cut up until the following April.

Exactly a month before the order to start work on No. 2290 was given, far to the west in the USA, from the Eddystone erecting shop of the Baldwin Locomotive Works there emerged another banker, or in this instance, pusher, by British standards a true giant. Comparing its leading dimensions with those of the Midland engine is an interesting exercise, though not to be taken too seriously. They were contemporaries, but there is no question of one being inherently inferior to the other, for they functioned in very different railway environments, the common features being their duties and the fact they were reciprocating steam locomotives running on standard gauge tracks.

	Midland Railway No. 2290	**Erie Railroad No. 2603**
Wheel arrangement	0-10-0	2-8-8-8-2
Cylinders	(4) 16¾in x 28in	(6) 36in x 32in
Coupled wheels	4ft 7½in	5ft 3in
Working pressure (both superheated)	180lb/in²	210lb/in²
Grate area	31½ft²	90ft²
Tractive effort	40765lb	160000lb
Loaded weight (engine and tender)	86 tons	426½ tons
Rigid wheelbase	20ft 11in	16ft 6in

Out of Susquehanna, New York & Erie Railroad trains heading east were faced with a winding 10 mile climb up to Gulf Summit, a section of track which in steam days kept helper engines busy, frequently added at both front and rear of freight trains. The company's first Mallets, three 0-8-8-0 tender locomotives of Class L1, entered service in the autumn of 1907, their specific assignment helping on the Susquehanna Hill. They were notable in being at the time of their introduction the largest locomotives in the world, despite which their 100ft² grates were hand fired, and also the only examples of their kind with the driver's cab mounted around the boiler; the 'Mother Hubbard.' They were identified by the Erie as the Angus type, after the well known immigrant Scots engineer Angus Sinclair, who was then employed by the company as a 'special instructor' and who is understood to have held a particular affection for it. In 1921 they were extensively modernised, single carrying axles were added fore and aft, and the cabs moved to the firebox end. In the meantime, however, something even larger had gone to work on the Susquehanna, the brainchild of George R. Henderson, a Baldwin consulting engineer. To his US Patent No. 1013771 of 1912, the Triplex concept was a variation on the idea of using tender weight to augment tractive effort (Chapter 4). Baldwin 41308 of April 1914, Erie Class P1No.2603 (later 5014), it carried the name *Matt H. Shay* on the cab side sheets (Not the Shay of geared logging locomotive fame, but a long serving Erie engineer (driver)). The six cylinders were all of the same diameter and stroke, but the locomotive functioned as a compound; to have fed live steam to all six cylinders one imagines would have drained the boiler in minutes. The two cylinders connected to the middle group of drivers received steam at high pressure directly from the boiler, the right hand exhausting at lower pressure to the front pair and the left to the rear. The latter vented separately to atmosphere via an outlet above the tender (visible in the painting). The Triplex arrangement raised the adhesive weight to 89% of the total engine weight, as compared to 65% for the L1 class as converted to 2-8-8-2 wheel arrangement. As a pusher, the new Triplex was considered to be the equal of three large eight-coupled locomotives, although on the downside, when it was shopped, these had to be sourced from elsewhere. It was tested hauling freight, and in fact was designed to be capable of shifting a 32000 ton train five miles in length, a concept that was never put to the test, though only because it was recognised it would have pulled out drawbars all along the train. No. 5014 did haul a 17912 ton load 1.6 miles long for 23 miles between Binghampton and Susquehanna, before a drawbar not unexpectedly failed. In the course of the run an attached dynamometer car had measured a maximum drawbar pull of 130000lb. However, in extended running it manifested the same shortcoming as its much smaller fellow banker on the Lickey, the inability of the boiler to keep up with the demands of the cylinders other than for relatively short periods. Too large to fit into the Erie's own shops, it received heavy repairs at the Sayre, Pennsylvania, establishment of the Lehigh Valley Railroad. Two further examples arrived from Baldwin in 1916, Nos. 5015 and 5016, differing only in detail, the trio pushing trains up to Gulf Summit until retired in 1927. They have frequently been described as failures, but this seems a little unfair. It is reasonable to suggest that for any operation other than pushing they were of limited value, and even for that it may be argued, as was so often the case in locomotive history, they were really too much for the job, but the fact remains that for a decade or more they were worked hard, kept the freight moving and so earned revenue for the railroad. The painting of No.5014 shows it on a typical day, the train's caboose coupled behind it as was normal practice. Placed in front of the giant Triplex, it would have been crushed.

Erie Power
F. Westing, A. Staufer 1991

The Mallet Locomotive
A.E. Durrant, David & Charles 1974

Midland Railway Locomotives Volume 4
S. Summerson, Irwell Press 2005

CHAPTER THIRTEEN

1916 NORTH BRITISH RAILWAY, UK
Beyer Peacock/NBR Cowlairs 2-6-0

The passenger on a train crossing the Forth Bridge today, looking to the west, will find the view dominated by the two road bridges (1964 and 2017), but in the first decade of the 20th Century the view along the north bank of the river would have been clear past Lower Craig and St Margaret's Hope to Rosyth Castle, where visible under construction by the contractor Easton, Gibb & Son was the extensive Rosyth Naval Dockyard. Approved in 1903, at an estimated cost of £3 million, the 1184 acre site had been chosen by the Admiralty as a convenient location from which to reach the North Sea, Germany beginning to replace France as a potential enemy. The construction workforce at its peak totalled 6000, but even so completion did not take place until 1916, well into World War 1. The berthing area was sufficient to accommodate eleven battleships, the first to receive dry dock attention being the 17500 ton King Edward Class *Zealandia*, built at Portsmouth Dockyard in 1905, but already rendered obsolete by the new Dreadnought type. It could, so it was said, 'neither fight nor run away', but survived the war, latterly as a depot ship, only to be scrapped almost immediately after. For a time, it was a part of the Rosyth-based Battle Cruiser Force under Sir David Beatty, to which were added in December 1917 the oil-fired steam powered twin funnel K Class submarines of Flotilla 13. Much vaunted by the Admiralty, but dangerous and ineffective, the so-called submersible destroyers were 340ft in length and displaced 1800 tons on the surface. When fully functioning they were capable of speeds not matched until the arrival of the modern nuclear submarine, but as one retired naval officer put it many years later, 'the only good thing about the K boats is that they never engaged the enemy.'

To properly service the needs of the vast Rosyth complex, its ships, their crews and the base workforce, a branch line was constructed over 1905-1907, leaving the Inverkeithing to North Queensferry pier goods line at Rosyth Naval Base Junction, a passenger station opening within the dockyard boundaries in July 1915. Easton & Gibb employed two 0-6-0 saddle-tanks, which on completion of the works were retained by the Admiralty, to be followed up to the end of World War 1 by five Barclay 0-4-0ST. More interesting from this period was London, Brighton & South Coast Stroudley 'Terrier' No.637 (Brighton 1878; No.37 *Southdown*; renumbered 637 1905). Sold along with three other members of the class to the Admiralty in February 1918 for use at Invergordon on the Moray Firth, it moved instead to Rosyth, where it spent little time and by June 1920 it was lying derelict at Ardrossan marked as Mine Depot Grangemouth No.5. This and the other locomotives were suited only for internal shunting, and in any case haulage on the branch line to Inverkeithing would have been in the hands of NBR 0-6-0 tender engines of varying capacity and because of wartime demands, greatly over-extended. There were not only heavy stores and coal trains to be worked, but the morning and evening workers' trains, which apart from serving stations in Fife, also ran to and from Edinburgh. In addition, the company would have had to find, as required, power for sailors' leave trains. In December 1918, the entire complement of the Grand Fleet was granted leave, moved by thirty-two specials from Rosyth and from Port Edgar, which lay almost opposite on the south bank (terminus of the South Queensferry branch). It is not surprising, bearing in mind additional wartime traffic across the entire NBR network, that by December the following year a full 22% of its locomotive stock had become unfit for work.

In 1895 the Midland & South Western Junction Railway acquired from the maker Beyer Peacock of Manchester a neat outside-cylinder 2-6-0 with 4ft diameter coupled wheels, intended for a South American customer but not delivered. Works number 3679, it became M&SWJR No.14, proving to be a valuable addition to the company's locomotive stock, to the extent that the following year a second example was purchased, Beyer Peacock 3884, M&SWJR No.16. The latter survived long enough to be given a GWR tender and Standard No.9 boiler in 1925, but was withdrawn five years later. No.14 had been taken out of use about the commencement of World War 1, its boiler being retained by the company for stationary use at Cheltenham, with the chassis going to the dealer Cashmore, in Cardiff. The exact sequence of events which followed, and the reasons lying behind them, are unrecorded, but at some point in 1915 the various parts of No.14 were reunited at the North British Railway's Cowlairs Works, with a view to returning it service. The boiler had to be condemned, but the chassis, obviously considered sufficiently useful to warrant rebuilding, was given a reconditioned NBR boiler, smokebox and standard cab, also provided with a spare tender. Thus restored to health, it was sent across the Forth to work trains between Rosyth Dockyard and Inverkeithing, possibly even further into Fife. It is discussed here under the heading of North British Railway, because without a doubt, as it worked outwith the Dockyard boundary, it would have been manned by NBR footplatemen, but it is not known what identity it carried, if any, or indeed in whose ownership it operated. It was never numbered in NBR stock, and it is possible that it was the Admiralty which took responsibility, responding to a desperate plea for assistance from the railway company, which in addition to having to cope with the huge volume of wartime traffic, between 1917 and 1919 had to cover for the loss of twenty-five Holmes Class C goods engines, conscripted for service on the Western Front in France. Whatever the case, in this form, other than in the small diameter of its coupled wheels (the NBR goods standard was 5ft), the erstwhile No.14 is exactly the 2-6-0 the NBR might have had. Not, though, in its original form, which may be seen in the photograph opposite. Between 1882 and 1885, Beyer Peacock delivered seventy of these engines to the New South Wales Government Railways, Class 205 (later D205 and Z25), in their leading dimensions differing only fractionally from M&SWJR No.14; extremely reliable and primarily goods engines, they saw seasonal excursion work, running to schedules timed at 30mph. They were followed in 1889 by twenty-five engines to the same design from Dübs in Glasgow, Class B55 (Z24), which operationally were pooled with the Beyer Peacock group. No. 2510 of the latter is preserved at the New South Wales Rail Transport Museum, Thirlmere. No. 2413, Dübs 2635 of 1891, worked for the NSWGR until 1960, when it was withdrawn and sold to the State Electricity Authority for service at Bunnerong Power House, where it became No. 6. Finally taken out of use in 1975, it passed to the Australian Railway Historical Society, A.C.T. Division at Canberra, where it was photographed on 4 November 2000. Two years later it moved to a new home at Junee Roundhouse Museum. And what became of old No.14? As the war effort at Rosyth wound down, it was sold to the dealer J.F. Wake at Darlington, but that was not to be the end. In March 1918 Wake sold it on to the Cramlington Coal Company in Northumberland, where again rebuilt, though unchanged in appearance other than in the provision of deeper bufferbeams carrying additional low-set buffers, it ran as CCC No.15 until May 1929, when the company became a part of Hartley Main Collieries. Here it was known, in neat progression, as No. 16; the lower buffers were removed and it was paired with a different tender of older design, the springs inconveniently mounted inside the frames. In this form it remained until scrapped by the colliery company in August 1943, after a long, hard and useful career.

The Rosyth Dockyard branch survives. Presently without any traffic, it is perhaps retained in case needed, the Yard itself remaining an important defence asset, since 1997 operated by Babcock International. The painting, though, sees activity at its peak, No.14 heading in the direction of Inverkeithing with a lengthy train of miscellaneous passenger stock, crowded with workmen or even perhaps sailors beginning a spell of leave. Beyond the train is Rosyth Naval Base Junction, where the branch to North Queensferry pier (opened April 1878, closed October 1954) turns a little to the right, then quickly left over a bridge built to permit the newer Rosyth line to pass beneath. In the background is the Jamestown Viaduct carrying the 1890 main line up to the Forth Bridge, out of picture at left.

The Railways of Fife
W. Scott Bruce, Melven Press 1980

Mainline to Industry
F. Jones, Lightmoor Press 1998

Industrial Locomotives of Scotland
A. Bridges (editor) Industrial Railway Society 1975

A Compendium of New South Wales Steam Locomotives
A. Grumbach (compiler) ARHS NSW 1989

CHAPTER FOURTEEN

1918 NEW YORK, NEW HAVEN & HARTFORD RAILROAD USA

General Electric/Alco 2'AA+AA2' No. 068 (AC Electric)

To many, early main line railway electrification is associated with Europe, with Switzerland and Hungary, perhaps, but much of the credit really ought to go to the United States. In 1892 the newly formed General Electric Company signed an agreement with the Baltimore & Ohio Railroad to design and construct in its entirety the railroad's Baltimore Belt Line, on which some initial work had commenced in the previous year. Connecting the company's downtown Camden Station with its original Philadelphia line at Bay View Junction, it was steeply graded and included the 7340 ft long tunnel beneath Howard Street, over which the city authorities would not permit ventilation shafts or fans because of the detrimental effect they would have on the amenity of an already built up area. North of the tunnel, the line turned east through the residential area of Peabody Heights (up and coming) and Waverly (old established). When construction began the B&O had no clear idea of how it was going to operate this section of railroad, though in deciding on electric traction in practice it had little choice (cable traction was considered). Nonetheless, it was an act of considerable courage on the part of both parties concerned, as the form then had not progressed much beyond streetcar systems. The line opened in the spring of 1895, initially with steam traction in both directions, but electric locomotives took over in May of the following year, though, as always intended, in one direction only. Westbound, the grade was in favour of trains, permitting steam locomotives to drift down into the city, the electric locomotives working eastbound. Two would be coupled at the head of the train, with a steam locomotive attached behind them but not working, the procedure being that on the approach to the Waverly tower, the electric locomotives would cut off on the move and race ahead into a dead-end track between the main running lines. This pioneering operation, one that remained unusual to the end, lasted fifty-seven years, the power being switched off in 1952 following the arrival of new main line diesels. The electric locomotives when introduced in 1895 represented a huge leap forward, at 98 tons much larger and heavier than anything that had gone before. They had four quill-drive motors, each developing 360 hp, powering four 5ft 2in wheels set in an articulated frame, well able to meet the design requirement of hauling 500 ton passenger trains upgrade at 35 mph or 1500 ton freight trains at 15 mph. Initially, power collection was through what has been described as an 'overhead third-rail', into which would slot a metal shoe extending up from the locomotive's roof. Cumbersome, it proved unsatisfactory and in 1902 was replaced by the straightforward ground level arrangement.

Other pioneers of main line electrification in the USA deserving of mention are the Pennsylvania Railroad (1905), Chicago, Milwaukee & St Paul (1916) and the New York, New Haven & Hartford (1907). It is the last named which is our present concern, a railroad which in its day ran an exceptionally diverse range of motive power and stock, despite owning rather less mileage than most US Class 1 companies. What it did have was electricity, beginning in 1895 with the conversion to overhead wire DC traction of the Nantasket Junction to Pemberton line, followed in 1907 by the pioneering introduction of 11000V AC, initially between Cos Cob and Woodlawn. The early DC electrification had come about as the result of competition from streetcar and interurban lines, involving the conversion to overhead wire of eleven routes and to third-rail of five. All but one had ceased operation by 1935, defeated largely by bus and private car, the exception being the eight mile stretch between Stamford and New Canaan, which in 1908 sensibly was converted to AC operation as it was a short branch off the company's main line. In New York the NYNH&H used New York Central & Hudson River trackage to access Grand Central station, from which, under a City ordinance, steam locomotives were banned effective 1 July 1908. The response of the NYC&HR was to electrify on the third-rail system at 650V DC, its trains thus powered reaching NYNH&H metals at Wakefield (just beyond Woodlawn) in July 1907. The New Haven, forced to consider how its trains henceforth would reach Grand Central, concluded that the only sensible option from an operating and economic point of view would be to electrify the entire main line, initially as far as Stamford (outer limit of suburban traffic), but as soon as possible out to New Haven. It was well aware from its own experience that voltage drop with direct current would render it unsuited to long distance operation of heavy main line locomotives and multiple unit trains. In 1905, on the recommendation of the company's Electrical Engineer, W.S. Murray, the NYNH&H announced to a startled and doubting railroad world its innovative decision to electrify at 11000V AC, single-phase, Westinghouse to supply thirty-five locomotives of B-B wheel arrangement, also the power plant and transmission equipment. It is difficult to overstate the challenge which faced the two companies; alternating current at the time was scarcely employed commercially, while the locomotives, for example, would not only have to connect with AC overhead 22 ft above rail, but also run on the DC third rail inward of Wakefield, the changeover to be made without stopping. Naturally there were teething troubles, but the planners were vindicated. Electric operation along the initial section commenced on 18 April 1907, the New Canaan and Harlem River branches being added in 1908 and 1912 respectively, the four-track main line onward from Stamford to New Haven in 1915 and from there the short distance on to the Cedar Hill freight yards in 1917. At the other end of the line, the wires crossed the Hell Gate Bridge in 1917, reached along the South Norwalk to Danbury branch in 1925 and finally to Bay Ridge (freight) in 1927. In all, electric trains covered 152 route miles, but taking into account yards and sidings, 673 track miles.

Local passenger services were operated by a large fleet of multiple-unit trains, but for longer distances and for freight, a total of 189 locomotives was employed, the last new examples being introduced in 1956-1957, a decade before the NYNH&H ceased to exist. The fleet was built up in batches, 41 in 1906-1908, 96 in 1912-1928, 26 in 1931-1943 and finally 21 in 1955-1957. The majority of the earlier locomotives came from Baldwin-Westinghouse, with GE-Alco suppling seven in 1926. But from that year on, other than five from the former in 1942, the remainder were GE products only. Over time these locomotives served the New Haven well, in particular the ten box-cab Class EP-2 2`C+C2` passenger locomotives, highly successful machines which in effect formed the basis of the Pennsylvania Railroad's world famous GG-1. Not included in the total so far, however, are five early 'experimentals'. Four, Nos.069-072, came from Baldwin-Westinghouse in 1910-1911 and the fifth, No.068, pictured here, from GE-Alco. It is believed to have been completed in 1912, but probably did not reach New Haven metals until 1915. Of 2`AA+AA2` wheel arrangement, it was equipped with series-repulsion motors, adopting a form used in Europe by AEG and in Britain by the London, Brighton & South Coast Railway for its South London electrification of 1909, to promote which the company adopted the North American description Elevated Electric. No.068 had four motors, each geared to a jackshaft connected to one pair of 4ft 6in diameter uncoupled driving wheels. Maximum continuous output was 1560hp. Although apparently intended to be dual-voltage, it was not delivered as such, lacking shoes for third-rail running, and was always regarded by the NYNH&H purely as a freight locomotive. Not considered worthy of development, nonetheless it did remain on the roster for over a decade, until condemned in 1928.

The painting shows No.068 on a Sunday work train, passing the New Haven's electricity generating station at Cos Cob, to the west of Stamford. A massive plant, the south side of which, facing on to Long Island Sound, was styled in a manner designed to avoid offence to the more sensitive souls on passing luxury yachts. The electrification's massive infrastructure is clearly evident, in particular the robust design of the overhead, the two parallel messenger wires supporting a single contact wire, creating the form of a triangle. The arrangement rose out of the belief that the ideal combination was rigid catenary and flexible pantograph, but it proved expensive to install and maintain (as the LBSCR was to find, having adopted the same system for its South London electrification) and was not employed when the wires were extended towards New Haven. It may be said, however, that the New Haven's electrification, carried out from 1907, physically and commercially, as an enterprise truly was colossal.

New Haven Power 1838-1968
J.W. Swanberg, A.F. Staufer 1995

Royal Blue Line
H.H. Harwood Jnr, Greenberg Publishing 1990 (B&O history)

The LBSCR Elevated Electrification, A Pictorial View of Construction
S. Grant, Noodle Books 2011

Stephenson Locomotive Society Journal
894 Jul/Aug 2015 (An Enigmatic Electric, R.A.S. Hennessey)
895 Sep/Oct 2015 (postscript to above, A.M. Levitt)

CHAPTER FIFTEEN

1920 VISIMU-UTKINSK RAILWAY, RUSSIA
Glover 2-8-0 *КОММУНИСТ* 884mm Gauge

In the author's earlier years Russia, the controlling force in the Soviet bloc of nations, was almost a closed book, but from time to time a page would open to reveal a tantalising glimpse of what was inside. Often, as we now know, this would mislead; within there might be formations of exotic aircraft over Tushino, exciting western observers, but then never seen again, and other manifestations of military might designed to deceive. In the West, there was self-serving talk of Soviet superiority in bomber aircraft and ballistic missiles, with from time to time public amusement resulting from the unveiling as a spy of a pillar of the British establishment. Information on Russian railways, at least since the Revolution, similarly was scarce, only the occasional grainy picture appearing in print, the image frequently partially wiped by early airport x-ray machines, with from time to time officially promoted publicity concerning some new development. It was known of course that it was a land where steam locomotive classes attained numbers unheard of anywhere else, other than by the wartime German Type 52. As to books, the first worthwhile publication purchased by the author, having decent sharp photographs, was Le Fleming and Price's Russian Steam Locomotives of 1960. Their remark "It is a sobering thought that one single class of Russian locomotive is barely less than the entire steam stock of British Railways" made a profound impression (the reference was to the E series 0-10-0 built over a period of 45 years from 1912, and today calculated to have totalled above 11000 examples). For its time, it was a commendably thorough work, but unable to say much about such singularities as the lone Beyer-Garratt exported from Britain in 1932 ('dismantled in 1937') and the unique, unusable AA20-1 of 1934, the world's sole 4-14-4, its appearance made familiar through the medium of heavily retouched photographs (fate 'unknown'). In fact, surprisingly and creditably, the former remained active in eastern Siberia until as recently as 1957, while the latter was left to rust at the Shcherbinka test centre for a quarter of a century, not being cut up until 1960; a massive failure in every sense. It does seem a shame it was not preserved, for it would have made a magnificent museum exhibit.

All the above ran on the Russian standard gauge of 1524mm (today 1520mm). Although it was known a vast narrow gauge network also existed, information concerning the post-1917 era was hard to come by. Except, that is, for the various so-called Pioneer Railways, a creation of the USSR, their purpose both to imbue in young people an enthusiasm for the Communist ideal and, commendably, provide a practical basis for future careers. Frequently the subject of the official photographer, and thus quite well known in the West, they fascinated the author, who as a child thought them a jolly good idea; he would have made an eager Young Pioneer. The attraction was that the steam locomotives they employed were not purpose built, but of what might described as full-scale narrow-gauge type. The first narrow gauge railway proper in Russia ran 62km from Verhovye to Livny; of 1067mm gauge and opened in April 1871, it failed to set a precedent, largely due to poor construction. Real expansion of the narrow gauge did not commence until after 1892, following a decree which put in place a proper legal framework for the construction and operation of such railways as common carriers. During World War 1 the Russian army laid down extensive 750mm gauge field railways, while after 1928 there was a considerable expansion resulting from the Stalin industrialisation programme, although to some extent that had the contradictory effect of causing a number of narrow gauge systems to be relaid to 1524mm in order to cope with increased traffic. By the early 1960s, however, they covered something like 50000 km, mostly of 750mm gauge and in the service of industry. A few early locomotives had come from Britain, but the greatest quantity over the years were of German origin or design, though Russian workshops, in particular that at Kolomna, eventually successfully developed and produced large numbers.

Steam locomotives of North American origin on the Russian standard gauge were by no means unknown in both pre- and post-revolutionary Russia, the most familiar the famous YE 2-10-0, construction of which was divided between Alco and Baldwin. Initially a total of 1175 was ordered by the Russian Railway Mission, the intended destination the Trans-Siberian line, which in October 1915 assumed a vital strategic importance following Turkey's entry into the war on the side of the Central Powers, resulting in the loss to Russia of ports on the Black Sea. In 1917 a further 500 were ordered, but Revolution intervened and not all were delivered, a large number going to the US Army and later to railroads such as the Erie, where in general they appear to have been well regarded and useful machines. (2051 of a modernised version, very similar in appearance, again built by Alco and Baldwin, arrived in Russia during 1944-1945). The new ideological gulf between the two countries did nothing to dampen Russian admiration for US locomotive practice, and although Washington vetoed large orders, in October 1931 ten new locomotives arrived in Leningrad, five 2-10-4 from Alco and five 2-10-2 from Baldwin. They were more powerful than any previous Russian designs, and considerably heavier, so much so that they damaged the track and were not permitted to exceed 25km/h. Not repeated, they proved of value nonetheless, as a great deal that was useful was learned by Soviet engineers.

On the narrower gauges, steam locomotives were imported from the US in some numbers, just under 200 from six different makers being supplied between 1891 and 1918. The great majority were tank engines, but there were also a small number of 2-6-0 and 2-8-0 wheel arrangement and it is one of the latter which is the subject of the accompanying painting. In 1916 Vulcan Iron Works of Wilkes-Barre, Pennsylvania, supplied to the 875mm gauge Bogoslovsk – Sos'va railway two straightforward 2-8-0 locomotives, works numbers 2547-2548, running numbers 31 and 32. Cylinders were 381mm by 508mm and coupled wheels 915mm. Sometime in the 1920s No. 31 was transferred to the Visimo-Utkinsk system, the gauge of which was a nominal 9mm greater. It was withdrawn in 1961, but may have stopped work earlier, as in 1960 the gauge was narrowed to the common 750mm. The railway ran 64 km north-east from the works complex at Visimo-Utkinsk to Nizhny Tagil, which lies in the industrial Urals about 200 km east of Perm and 120 km north-west of Sverdlovsk. The 2-8-0 illustrated is one of two delivered to the same company in 1920, but from a different maker, the Glover Machine Works, of Marietta, Georgia. Dimensionally they matched exactly the Vulcan engines, other than in cylinder bore, which was 355.6mm (all four weighed 36.32 tons). Works numbers 142011-142012, for '34.8in' gauge, they were ordered in 1916 by Paul Demidoff of the San Donato Mining & Iron Works, Petrograd, although this was an administrative address (Petrograd became Leningrad in 1924, but today has reverted to the original St Petersburg).

The Revolution caused delay, but the order was not cancelled and in October 1920 the two locomotives were shipped from Philadelphia. To emphasise there was a new order in Russia, 142011 was named *КОММУНИСТ* (Communist) and 142012 *ИНТЕРНАЦИОНАЛИСТ* (Internationalist), cyrillic lettering applied at Marietta prior to dispatch, Glover's painters no doubt working to very precise instructions. One wonders how the work came to Glover, and bearing in mind virtually identical dimensions, whether perhaps the four had been ordered together by Demidoff, the Visimo-Utkinsk pair being passed on by a hard-pressed Vulcan, coping with a full order book. Just as had Filer & Stowell and Dewey Bros., Glover entered business supplying machinery to the lumber industry, commencing the construction of railway locomotives at the request of established customers. The first was Glover 8141 (works numbers did not run in sequence), a 3ft gauge 0-4-0ST of 1902, and the last 101440, fittingly of the same type and gauge, in 1930. In between, around 200 locomotives to a wide variety of designs were constructed for customers in the USA and abroad, largely the Caribbean and South America. After 1930 the company continued to produce machinery at Marietta, but the complex was demolished in 1995 when a move was made 130 miles south to Cordele. For those who wish to learn more, the story of Glover locomotives is told in Richard Hillman's fascinating and generously illustrated account (see below).

Glover Steam Locomotives, The South's Last Steam Builder
R.L. Hillman, Heimburger House 1996

Narrow Gauge Steam Locomotives - Russia
L. Moskalev / V. Bochenkov / S. Dorozhkov, Moscow Publishing House 2012

Russian Steam Locomotives
H. M. Le Fleming / J.H. Price, John Marshbank Limited 1960

Narrow Gauge Steam Locomotives in Russia and the Soviet Union
K.R. Chester (Ed.), Trackside Publications 2003

CHAPTER SIXTEEN

1924 LONDON, MIDLAND & SCOTTISH RAILWAY, UK
Hookham Class 3F 0-6-0 No. 2367

The universally employed and affectionate nickname of the North Staffordshire Railway, one which long-survived it, was 'The Knotty' (after the Stafford Knot symbol widely used by the company; a representation of the simple overhand knot, it apparently pre-dated the mediaeval period, later being adopted by the de Stafford family). From its formal opening in April 1848 until absorbed into the new giant London, Midland & Scottish Railway in July 1923, its own rails remained confined to a geographically small area, but through the development of positive relationships with adjacent companies its freight locomotives reached as far as Liverpool and passenger Llandudno in North Wales. A Punch cartoon of 1850 titled 'Station on the North Staffordshire Line' depicts an intending passenger being advised by a youthful figure lounging against a door; yes, he was indeed the ticket clerk, but that as to the departure time of the London train, "Oh, I don't know. No time in pertickler. Sometimes one time – and sometimes another." It suggests operations got off to an uncertain start, but the fact remains that for all its small size, the NSR became an institution, a great servant of the Potteries and outlying districts, and a profitable one at that. From 1888 the annual dividend on ordinary stock rarely fell below 4%, and in the later years reached 5%.

Although it reached into attractive rural countryside, the heart of the NSR lay in The Potteries, in the six towns of Burslem, Fenton, Hanley, Longton, Tunstall and Stoke-upon-Trent, in 1910 gathered together unwillingly as the city of Stoke-on-Trent (Arnold Bennett it seems deliberately omitted Fenton because he he thought 'Five Towns' rolled off the tongue more easily than 'Six'). The North Stafford's passenger operations thus were to a great extent local in nature, the only regular services of any length running between Crewe and Derby via Stoke, for which reason there was a limited requirement for passenger tender locomotives. Class 19 consisted of three small 2-4-0s of 1905-1906, used for the seasonal Derby to Llandudno expresses until the arrival of four G and one KT Class 4-4-0 in 1910-1912, which also took charge of the heavier trains between Crewe and Derby, the 2-4-0s

40

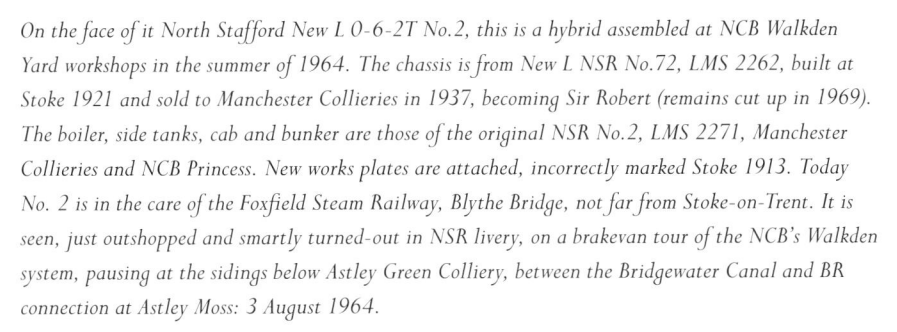

On the face of it North Stafford New L 0-6-2T No.2, this is a hybrid assembled at NCB Walkden Yard workshops in the summer of 1964. The chassis is from New L NSR No.72, LMS 2262, built at Stoke 1921 and sold to Manchester Collieries in 1937, becoming Sir Robert (remains cut up in 1969). The boiler, side tanks, cab and bunker are those of the original NSR No.2, LMS 2271, Manchester Collieries and NCB Princess. New works plates are attached, incorrectly marked Stoke 1913. Today No. 2 is in the care of the Foxfield Steam Railway, Blythe Bridge, not far from Stoke-on-Trent. It is seen, just outshopped and smartly turned-out in NSR livery, on a brakevan tour of the NCB's Walkden system, pausing at the sidings below Astley Green Colliery, between the Bridgewater Canal and BR connection at Astley Moss: 3 August 1964.

When the author first visited the area, the landscape appeared almost as it had been for a century or more, one of tall chimneys, pit-head winding gear, colliery waste tips, slag banks and kilns, but the end was not far off. Even so, he was able to see locomotives built locally at Black Bull by Robert Heath & Sons still at work, alongside much younger examples from Bagnalls of Stafford. Pictured during one of his later visits, in March 1968, NCB No.3 (Bagnall 2992/ 1950) stands in steam at Parkhouse Colliery, Chesterton, ready for such little work as remained, for the mine closed two months later. The smoking chimneys, which belong to the Metallic Tile Company, are rather taller than they appear, for the land drops away sharply beyond the colliery sidings, hiding from view the BR Chesterton branch, which closed at the same time as the mine.

---

finishing their lives along the Churnet Valley. The short distance stopping trains were in the hands of tank locomotives gradually increasing in size from 2-4-0 and 2-4-2 (the latter rebuilds of the former), to 0-4-4, 4-4-2 and finally 0-6-4, together with a fleet of mixed traffic 0-6-2s. Goods services were taken care of by the characteristic British inside-cylinder 0-6-0, both tender and tank. Few NSR locomotives of later years had cylinders outside the frames, but they included five products of local maker Kerr Stuart, two 0-6-0T (NSR 74-75, LMS 1602-1603) intended for Argentina but not shipped, and three steam railmotors, the engine units of 0-2-2T arrangement (NSR and LMS 1-3, withdrawn 1927). There were three 3ft 6in gauge 0-4-0ST at the company owned Caldon Low Quarry (*Frog* and *Toad* by Hughes of Loughborough, 1877, and *Bobs* by Bagnall of Stafford, 1901; all scrapped in May 1936). To be included in the total also were two attractive 2-6-4T by Kitson of Leeds on the 2ft 6in gauge Leek & Manifold Light Railway, which was an associate company of and operated by the North Stafford (L&M and LMS 1 *E R Calthrop* and 2 *J B Earle*) The line was closed in March 1934 and the locomotives scrapped in 1937. The only other NSR locomotive with two outside cylinders also had two inside the frames, the unique No. 23, the subject of the drawing.

The last Locomotive Superintendent of the NSR was J.A. Hookham, previously Works Manager at Stoke, who had a solid locomotive and engineering background. Appointed in 1915 on the death of his predecessor, he had only eight years in post before his company's independent existence came to an end. During his tenure, with the exception of No. 23, new construction was limited to updated examples of existing designs, four Class New M 0-4-4T, six Class F 0-6-4T and twelve Class New L 0-6-2T, two of which, Nos.1 and 2 of 1923, were the last locomotives delivered to the North Stafford. After withdrawal in November 1937, the pair, together with three others of the same class were sold to Manchester Collieries Ltd at Walkden, where they worked for over two decades (the history of No.2, latterly LMS 2271, is not straightforward – see above). Hookham was truly only able to express himself through No.23, a compact 0-6-0T, Class D, with four 14in by 24in cylinders in line beneath the smokebox, each having its own set of Walschaerts valve gear, the outside and inside cranks placed at 90 degrees to one another, with the outside and inside cranks on the same side at 135 degrees. This provided more uniform torque and even firebox draught, which together with the fact that the entire weight of just under 57 tons bore on the small 4ft 6in coupled wheels, was intended to give the reliable adhesion and sharp acceleration required for the company's more difficult local services. No. 23 was tested on a number of different routes around Stoke, on occasion equipped with an indicator shelter attached over the front end, but with indifferent results, in part at least due to steaming difficulties. In the light of this, it is surprising that in what must have been one of the earlier decisions of the new Midland Railway dominated locomotive department, No.23 was permitted to be converted into a tender locomotive, not simply a matter of removing the side tanks, but requiring extensive alteration at the rear end. The tender provided appears to have been from one of the old Class 19 2-4-0s withdrawn in 1920. So rebuilt, it took up a regular turn working goods between Stoke and Colwich, but for only a short period, during which it was allocated three different numbers by the LMS, 1599, 2367 and 8689, although the first was never carried. The end came in December 1928, when it was finally set aside. In the drawing it is seen, not on its regular run, but approaching Stoke from the north, having just passed the station at Longport.

North Staffordshire Album
G. Dow, Ian Allan 1970

The Knotty, An Illustrated Survey of the North Staffordshire Railway
B. Jeuda, Lightmoor Press 1996

The Iron, Steel and Coal Industry in North Staffordshire
A.C. Baker, Irwell Press 2003

British Locomotive Catalogue 1825-1923 Volume 4
B. and D. Baxter (compilers), Moorland Publishing 1988 NSR Locomotive List

CHAPTER SEVENTEEN

1929 DEUTSCHEN VERSUCHSANSTALT FÜR LUFTFAHRT GERMANY
Propeller Drive Test Vehicle

Speed in comparatively recent times has become something of an end in itself, a resort of thrill seekers, mostly though not exclusively male. If, though, we look back to the beginnings of wheeled passenger transport in Britain, we find a rather different attitude. Shortening the time taken between two points had a specific purpose, to ease the strain of what one mid-17th Century traveller described in a letter to a friend as "a disgusting and tedious labour", or another similarly as "sitting from five in the morning till almost nine at night, plunging in the cold and dirt and dark, and that for two whole days in strange company." William Kitchener, in his book The Traveller's Oracle or Maxims for Locomotion, published in 1828, noted that as early as 1660 coaches were operating on a regular basis, recording that John Crossell of Charter House tried his best to write them (coaches) down, because he had "the countenance of the country gentlemen, who were afraid if their wives could get easily and cheaply to London, they might not settle so well afterwards to their domestic duties at the Hall or Grange." Pent-up demand lay behind John Palmer's introduction to a 16hr schedule of his Bristol to London fast mail, starting in 1784, while canals put on so-called fly-boats which attained speeds of up to 10mph. The poor, who travelled little and only of absolute necessity, made do with riding amidst a heap of parcels and packages on the waggons which plied most main roads. It was the first two decades of the 19th Century that brought greatly improved speed and comfort to road travel, through the graded surfaces of 'Blind Jack' Metcalfe, Thomas Telford, and from 1816 of J.L. McAdam. The advance is illustrated by another, evocative passage from Kitchener's book, concerning the Holyhead Mail, which in 1800 departed London at eight in the evening and arrived at Shrewsbury between ten and eleven the following night, taking 27 hours for 162 miles. "This distance is now done (1828) in 16¼ hours and the Mail is actually at Bangor ferry, 83 miles further, in the same time it used to take in reaching the post-office at Shrewsbury. We fancy we now see it, as it was when we travelled on it in our schoolboy time – the road in those days loose uncovered sand in part – with Charles Peters or old Ebden quitting his seat as guard and coming to the assistance of the coachman, who had flogged his horses until he could flog them no longer. We think we see them crawling up the hill into Shrewsbury town – whip – whip – whip – and an hour behind their time by the clock. It is now a treat to see them approach the town, if not before, never after the minute."

Then, in 1830, came the world's first inter-city railway, the Liverpool & Manchester. The reaction of existing travellers, the well to-do at least, was mixed for a number of reasons, one of them the fact that by that date coach travel in many respects had become quite civilised and, in the opinion of many, perfectly acceptable in terms of comfort. Early passenger trains did indeed give a poorer ride than coaches running on the better roads; Thomas Tredgold, a noted writer on railway matters, said, of his experience on the L&M, "The carriage rocks like a ship at sea, whilst at every swing one wheel or the other strikes a rail with considerable violence. Springs have they, but they spring not." First and second class rail travellers were nonetheless treated with care, company servants strictly controlling access and ensuring the lower orders boarded the open trucks provided. The youthful London & South Western Railway made its opinion of the latter crystal clear by forcing them to purchase their tickets at a booking hole labelled For Horses, Dogs & Third Class Passengers. At least one member of the female sex was entranced. The estimable young actress Fanny Kemble, then 21 years old, took to rail travel with zest, having captivated George Stephenson and been treated to a footplate ride on *Rocket*. Afterward, she told a friend how thrilled she had been and of how she had removed her bonnet, letting her hair "free to the wind." Carriage stock did improve fairly quickly, but track less so, and the early advantage of rail was not so much speed in itself, but the ability to run non-stop over longer distances and transport both people and goods in bulk. However, inevitably, the pace of everyday life was quickened by the railways, one early manifestation of which was the public enthusiasm for day excursions. But what we now regard as high-speed train travel arose through competition from other modes, when road and air transport established themselves in a meaningful way, and to a more limited extent from other train operators running between the same destinations.

Britain remained faithful to steam for its most prestigious passenger services, partly through simple resistance to change and partly because it had abundant quantities of coal to hand, but other countries, where conditions were otherwise, looked to alternatives. Germany is taken here for illustration. Following isolated experiments with prototype steam locomotives and electric railcars which reached speeds above 210km/h in 1903, it was not until 1933, initially with the 160km/h two-car diesel-electric SVT 877, the *Flying Hamburger*, that regular, high-speed services in any number began meeting a real demand for fast links between major centres of population. They were useful also as a means by which the Reichsbahn could demonstrate continued relevance, in competition as it was with other modes and in the face of high-level political indifference. The new multiple unit trains confirmed that reliable forms of transmission had been achieved. It had been, in part, concern for this aspect of high-speed operation that led the engineer Franz Kruckenberg of Heidelberg in 1926 to take out his Patent No.433457 for an underslung monorail, having an airship-shaped passenger cabin and driven by propellers at either end, speeds of up to 360km/h being envisaged. After further consideration, however, he concluded that this method of propulsion could be more readily and cost-effectively applied to a vehicle running on a conventional railway. In order both to test the theory, and develop more advanced models, in April 1928 he formed the Flugbahn-Gesellschaft (Flight Railway Company), the same year reaching agreement with DRG to make use of the 8km Isernhagen – Grössburgwedel section north-east of Hannover, which was straight, passed through empty countryside on the southern fringe of the Lüneburg heath, and at the time carried no regular traffic. By coincidence, DVL, the Deutschen Versuchsanstalt für Luftfahrt (German Experimental Institute for Aviation) had at its Berlin-Adlershof premises the four-wheel propeller driven rail vehicle which is the subject of these paintings. It had been constructed twelve years previously, but the Institute, concerned that now aviation technology in Germany was falling behind other countries, was seeking a decent length of railway along which it could conduct high-speed research into aircraft propeller design. Two BMW IV motors of 230hp mounted fore and aft drove two-blade propellers; total weight was 12.5 tonnes. Early in 1929 it was taken into the Reichsbahn repair shops at Leinhausen where extensive test instrumentation was installed, to suit the needs both of the Kruckenberg team and the Institute's researchers. The jointly operated test runs it would seem went well. Although the drag-inducing shape of the vehicle restricted it to a maximum of 175km/h, it rode smoothly at all speeds, other than a spell of vibration at 130km/h. The test crew monitoring the instruments were enclosed in a central compartment, but the driving position was in the roof and open to the elements, in certain side wind conditions apparently causing serious discomfort to its occupants. After 82 test runs totalling 1000km, this predecessor of the famous 'Propellerwagen', or 'Schienenzeppelin', returned to Berlin Adlershof, but saw no further use, and is believed to have been reduced to scrap soon after. Plans for a second DVL rail vehicle, drawn up at the same time, came to naught. What did materialise in 1930, however, was Franz Kruckenberg's record breaking, 20-passenger *'Schienenzeppelin'*. With its 26m long silver body and rear mounted propeller, it achieved world wide fame, and remains to this day widely recognised.

Two of the paintings show side and end-on aspects, the third, lower right (from a photograph) a method of testing which today would not for one moment be countenanced. In 1929, one imagines, it was simply accepted as necessary. The leading members of Franz Kruckenberg's team in 1929-1930 were Fritz Heyner, Curt Stedefeld and Willy Black. It is Black, engineer and enthusiastic supporter of the project, who we see here lashed with ropes to the suspension, keeping a close eye on the high speed wheel/rail interface. There is every chance that when he went home that evening he told his wife, or his friends perhaps, that it had been just an average day at work.

Der Schienenzeppelin
A. Gottwald, EK-Verlag 2006
Deutsche Schnelltriebwagen
G. Dietz / P. Jauch, EK-Verlag 2003
Quarterly Review Volume XXCVI, December 1832
(extracts from **The Traveller's Oracle or Maxims for Locomotion** *W Kitchener MD London 1828)*

CHAPTER EIGHTEEN

1931 LIMBURGSCHE TRAMWEG-MAATŚCHAPPIJ NETHERLANDS

Henschel 0-6-0+0-6-0 No. 51 (Garratt Type)

From the late 19th Century until World War 1 the steam tramway and roadside light railway could be found all across France (touched upon in Chapter 8), Belgium and the Netherlands. Serious and often terminal damage to many occurred during that War, and for those that survived life became ever more difficult thereafter, the bus and lorry denuding them of most of their business. One of those that did manage to continue was the Rotterdamsche Tramweg Maatśchappij with both standard and 1067mm gauge tracks. On the latter it operated a substantial fleet of steam locomotives, some fully enclosed, others having only skirtings, including fourteen attractive little 0-6-0 well tanks of 1905-1908 by Dutch maker Werkspoor. Some worked until 1961, although partially replaced by locally made diesel locomotives with substantial and distinctive wooden bodywork. The trains were gradually squeezed out by road traffic, but a serious blow from which the narrow gauge lines never really recovered was the great flood of 1953 that either submerged or left isolated three-quarters of the system, the last of which struggled on until 1966. All Dutch steam tramways had a special charm of their own, best epitomised perhaps in a photograph of an Orenstein & Koppel 0-8-0T (12000/1929) on the 750mm gauge Geldersche system, heading a freight train through the narrow streets of Doetinchem and about to make a sharp right turn, with a small shop to one side and pantiled roofed houses to the other. The company's No.26, it bore the name *Mr. J.P. Coops*, the inclusion of the masculine title a delightful touch which to the author summed up perfectly his idea of the Dutch character, formal and unfailingly polite. The Geldersche operated 56km of line, Arnhem – Doetinchem – Genderingen and on to

44

Isselburg in Germany; opened in 1881, it ran a passenger service until 1926 and goods with steam power until 1949; closure came in 1957.

The tramway development in the Netherlands began at the end of the 1870s, finance coming largely from private funds (the word Maatschappij here is best translated as Company). The main conditions attached to their construction were that maximum speed should not exceed 15km/h (raised in 1889 to 20km/h), and they must not make physical connection with main line railways, even where of the same gauge. In addition, as by and large their rails ran at the side of roads, they had to pay tolls, although had considerable freedom in setting fares and service levels. Their location placed them under the provincial rules governing road traffic, but gave complete freedom from railway regulations. Locomotives had to be at least partially enclosed, and in 1910 further guidance as to design was provided by the then chief inspecting officer Dr. Verhoop. The desiradata he listed as: (1) normal speed 35km/h, but to be easily capable of 50km/h, (2) simple construction, (3) easy to maintain, (4) economical on fuel, (5) easy for one man to control, (6) to pull on level track 160 tonnes, (7) to have adequate water capacity with low centre of gravity, (8) to be superheated and to have a feed water heater (the latter to his design). Four track gauges were to be found, the most widely used being 1067mm, followed closely by 1435mm, then 1000mm, 750mm and finally, on just one system, 700mm. This was the exposed 4.2km Den Helder – Huisduinen line which crossed the bleak spit of land at the northern tip of West Friesland, facing the narrow sea passage between it and the island of Texel. Operating in summer only, it opened in 1896, closed in 1907, reopened in 1911, then expired finally in 1917. It had three tiny 0-4-0T, Nos.1 and 2 by Backer & Rueb of Breda (121-122/1896), built with vertical boilers which were later replaced by the horizontal variety, and No.3, of straightforward design, by Maffei (3837/1913). On closure, the first two were sold to the dealer H.Vlot of Maastricht and scrapped in 1922, while No.3 soldiered on in industrial service for a number of years, latterly as No.1 at the Smulders & Teulings brickworks in Tilburg.

The system specifically under discussion is LTM, Limburgsche Tramweg-Maatschappij, which operated in Limburg province, that part of far south east Netherlands which somehow squeezes itself in between Belgium to the west and Germany to the east. A late example of its kind, the 1000mm gauge Centrale Limburgsche Spoorweg (Stoomtramweg) Maatschappij, opened in 1915, employed a fleet of 19 steam locomotives, all 0-4-0T, all of German origin. Its trackage, which lay in the Horn, Venlo and Roermond districts, was taken over in 1921 by the LTM, which at the same period also absorbed a local Venlo system and the Limburgche Electrische Spoorweg Maatschappi, a standard gauge company with 5km of track connecting Heerlen and Honsbroek. This had also worked under contract a line belonging to the Staatsmijmem (state coal mines), employing eight four-coupled steam locomotives, which were not transferred to LTM ownership. From 1921 the latter constructed two separate groups of standard gauge tracks of 40.7km and 27.5km in length. The latter section was a true light railway rather than a tramway, including some substantial earthworks and a lengthy steel viaduct at Gulpen, junction for a 2.5km branch to Wijlre, but as an investment ill-judged. Indeed, it is remarkable that by this date it was ever considered to be a worthwhile undertaking, and unsurprisingly, apart from a section which was electrified in 1923, it ceased operating in 1937. The steam locomotive fleet, none of fully enclosed tram type, was a mixed group, as follows; sixteen 0-4-0T, Nos. 21-35 (Hanomag 9857-9866/1922 and 10209-10213/ 1925) and No.64, Henschel (17698/1920), acquired second hand; three 0-6-0T, Nos. 51-52 (Linke Hoffman 2542 and 2547/1922) and No. 53 (Krupp 737/1924), also second hand; finally, last but not least, one of the most interesting Garratt-type locomotives ever constructed, the second No.51.

The story and success of the Garratt form of articulation is well known and does not require repeating here, suffice to say that the wheel arrangement of No.51, 0-6-0+0-6-0 was rare, and that in certain other respects this particular locomotive was unique. (The first LTM No.51 had been sold in 1923). The LTM order was placed with Hannoversche Maschinenfabrik AG of Hannover-Linden (Hanomag), which allotted maker's number 10758, but before assembly was completed the company was taken over by Henschel of Kassel, which numbered it 22063 in its own series. The design was carried out under the direction of Dr. Verhoop, at this time Dutch state mechanical engineer. The total weight in working order of 71.5 tonnes fulfilled the requirement for a 70 tonne adhesive weight on a maximum axle load of 14 tonnes, the locomotive to be capable of negotiating S-shaped curves on a 20% upgrade. Wheels were 900mm diameter, four cylinders 360mm by 360mm, boiler pressure 12kg/cm² (171 lb/in²), grate area 2m², coal capacity 3 tonnes and water 7000 litres. Maximum tractive effort was 11900kg (26235 lb). In form it was what is commonly referred to as a Union Garratt, as the bunker was mounted on the main frame and not on the rear engine unit. The most interesting aspect of No.51's design was that the main frame, with boiler, cab and bunker, was mounted on two engine units identical to those of the 0-4-0T engines Nos. 21-35, with an additional axle added to each, the cylinders being between the frames, one feature which made this Garratt unique. Piston valves were actuated by Verhoop valve gear (see diagram). The purpose of this interesting arrangement was the sensible one of simplification of spares holdings. The location of the water tanks outside the wheels was not as inconvenient as might be inferred, as the low housings atop the engine units, containing the steam and exhaust pipes, also had lift up covers allowing easy access to the inside connecting rods and motion work. No.51 performed well, being a good steamer and running quietly without fuss up to its design speed of 40km/h, which makes it all the more unfortunate that its time on the LTM was so short. After closure of the line it was moved on three times, in the first two instances at least, sold, to Dotremont of Maastricht in 1938, to the Technical Office of 's-Gravenhage in 1940 and finally in 1941 to an unidentified destination in Germany, where it vanished in the fog of war. It was a sad end for an attractive and in so many ways fascinating locomotive.

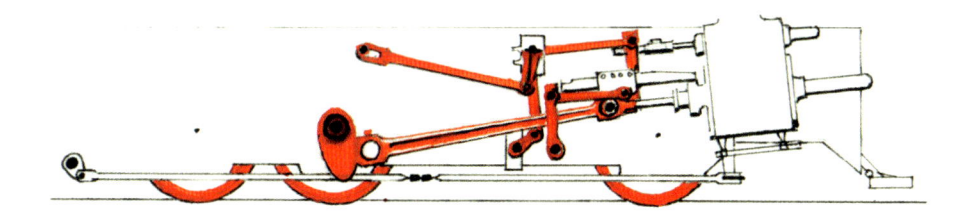

Layout of Verhoop valve gear, taken from a sectional elevation of LTM No.51. The view is between the frames, thus hiding the wheels and coupling rods, while the steam reverse also was not included. Here the cylinder is not shown in section. This form of gear equipped 16 types of Dutch steam tram locomotive. Of other gears the most widely employed was Joy (79), followed by Walschaerts (38), Stephenson (15), Allan (12), Belpaire (9), Brown (8) and Hackworth (2).

De Stoomlocomotieven de Nederlandse Tramwegen
S. Overbosch, De Bataafsche Leeuw 1985

The Continental Steam Tram
G.E. Baddeley, LRTA 1980

Narrow Gauge Railways of Europe
P. Allen / P.B. Whitehouse, Ian Allan 1959

CHAPTER NINETEEN

1937 QUEENSLAND RAILWAYS, AUSTRALIA
QR Ipswich RM 32 *Endeavour* (Petrol Engine Rail Motor) 1067mm Gauge

At Normanton in Yorkshire the traveller on the Midland Railway Scotch Express of 1876 would have taken – enjoyed may not be an accurate description – a thirty minute break for luncheon and for what we term today as 'comfort'. A six course meal was served in just twenty minutes, though one trusts not entirely eaten, while the carriages stood alongside the island platform and engines were changed, the running shed being conveniently located nearby. Standing on the Midland Railway main line between Sheffield and Leeds, and at a junction with that of the Lancashire & Yorkshire from Halifax and the west, it was an important and busy railway centre for many years, although the requirement for a refreshment stop in time disappeared. Today, a shadow of its former self, it remains rail served and connected to the national system, unlike its namesake, the Australian Normanton, which never was. It stands lonely in the Gulf Country of Queensland, and from it a single line of rails runs 94 miles south-eastward, separated by a full 306km from any other section of the 1067mm gauge Queensland Rail system (today distance on the Normanton line is uniquely measured in miles, all other QR lines in kilometres). Opened in 1885, it connected the river port of Normanton with Croydon at the foot of the Gregory Range of mountains, then the scene of a gold rush. In the past threatened with closure, the railway never did prosper, but today it survives, Heritage Listed, offering tourists a once weekly service, southbound on Wednesday, back on Thursday, seasonally from early April and 'weather permitting.' Remarkably, much of the trackage is the original light rail laid on hollow steel sleepers packed inside with mud and resistant to occasional flooding. The service is operated by Rail Motor Rmd 93, powered by a Gardner diesel engine, its body streamlined at the front and at the rear coupled to an unpowered trailer. Steam locomotives were used until 1922, in which year the characteristic and very useful petrol engine rail motors were introduced, adapted from AEC road chassis by the QR workshops. One of these was RM 80, later RM 32 *Endeavour*, which in 1929 was moved to Queensland's other totally isolated line, the Cooktown Railway.

Cooktown as a proper settlement was the creation in 1873 of the Queensland Government, the name chosen as here was the location where in 1770 Captain Cook had undertaken repair of his damaged vessel *Endeavour*. Its founding resulted from the discovery of gold 76 miles in a direct line to the south-west, around Maytown on the Palmer River, lying beyond the Great Dividing Range. Inevitably, there was a rush, Cooktown's population quickly expanding to 4000, while hordes headed west to the goldfield, often paying exorbitant sums for the carriage of belongings and supplies along the existing coach road, in dangerous conditions of heat and potential attack. Within three years Cooktown had become a recognised municipality, with sixty-two hotels, and at the goldfields around Palmer there were a further seventy-nine. While the rush itself dissipated quickly as the gold that was easily had was worked out, the field remained viable and production continued at a satisfactory level. Additionally, other activities developed, such as logging, sea cucumber fishing, grazing and agricultural farming. There was thus a necessity for reliable transportation between there and the coast at Cooktown, more than one scheme being put forward. A Transcontinental Railway from the east coast of south Queensland across the base of the northern peninsula to the great indentation of the Gulf of Carpentaria was proposed, creating a port there which would become the arrival point for mail steamers from Europe, linking at the Palmer with a line to Cooktown. It was not until November 1882 that the Queensland Parliament gave approval for a much less ambitious line from the east coast as far as Normanby, 32 miles, construction commencing in April 1884, the track to the Queensland standard 3ft 6in (1067mm). By the end of the year rails had been laid on the wharf at Cooktown and for 12½ miles inland, with bed prepared for a further 21 miles. Unfortunately adverse weather conditions caused difficulties and it was not until November the following year that the first section opened to Palmer Road, 31 miles from Cooktown. Two trains a week served intermediate stops at Marton, Jansen, Flaggy, Wilton, Coolah, Alderbury and Normanby, none of which initially had any buildings.

Maytown was the intended eventual destination, and in August 1885 a report prepared by the Chief Engineer, QR Carpentaria and Cook Divisions, pronounced on the respective advantages of two routes, one via Palmer and the other through the Lone Star Gap. In either case two substantial bridges would be required, over the Deighton and Laura rivers. However, despite the fact that after the 78 milepost the Lone Star Gap route would be mostly in cuttings and require seven tunnels, it would be 25 miles shorter than the Palmer and therefore was the favoured choice. The first locomotive on the line, other than the contractor's, was delivered new from Dübs in Glasgow (1922/1884) in January 1885. A 4-6-0 of QR Class F, Cooktown Railway No.1, it was intially hired out to assist in the construction work as far as Sandown, 51 miles from the start. On completion of that section in June 1887 it was returned to QR, but then hired again to cover the next 17 miles to Laura River, 68 miles from the sea, opened in October the following year. The extension towards Maytown was begun, the river at Laura crossed by means of a substantial 536½ft long iron lattice girder bridge of 80ft spans supported by six concrete piers. On 10th October 1891 it was tested for deflection by a locomotive and train totalling 90 tons, then never used again. Beyond, through the Great Dividing Range, no rails were ever laid, the Cooktown Railway entering a decline almost from the start. It covered its working expenses only in 1886 and 1888, but kept going until January 1903 when the Queensland Government, having failed to come to a leasing agreement with the Municipal Council, closed the line, a caretaker being taken on to safeguard the property. However, a revised offer was made and accepted, the Council reintroducing a thrice weekly service from 16 September, but as legislation required to permit it to do so legally had never been introduced, the Government resumed direct control from the start of the 1904-1905 financial year. With operating and maintenance costs kept to a minimum, the Cooktown thereafter quietly went about its business, largely unnoticed by the world outside, but in the absence of a decent parallel road, a servant of its community. World War 2 brought extra traffic, stores and equipment being required by military camps along the route, but time was running out and on 3 March 1962 the railway shut down for the last time. In the final five years of operation the average annual passenger carryings were around 1000 and goods tonnage 158.

In steam days on the Cooktown, 4-6-0 locomotives of classes B15 and PB15 (8 ton axle load), were permitted, but the only type regularly used was B13 (old Class F) of 6 ton axle load, the weight having been the heaviest permitted anywhere on the QR system up to 1913. Class B13 had 13in by 20in cylinders, 120lb/in² boiler pressure, and driving wheels 3ft 3in. Tractive effort at 80% boiler pressure was 8300lb, weight in working order, locomotive and tender, 50 tons. The first to run on the Cooktown was No.1, renumbered 199 in 1889, already mentioned, followed by three further examples up to the end of steam operation; No.2/200 (Dübs 2198/1886) was present between 1886 and 1917, No.3/201 (Dübs 2234/1887) between 1887 and 1899, and 190 (Kitson 2288/1885), on the line between 1900 and 1911. The last locomotive to arrive was a 2-6-0, Class B12 No. 40, another Dübs product (1136/1878), commencing work in October 1910 and after 1917 the only steam power on the railway, although seeing little use. It was withdrawn in 1927 and written off the books in March the following year. In 1916 the first Rail Motor entered service on the Cooktown, a 45 hp six-cylinder QR conversion of a Napier motor car which had already run 100,000 miles on roads. RM 6 *Captain Cook*, it carried 12 including the driver, but normally ran with two open sided trailers accommodating 16 passengers or goods (they had roofs and canvas blinds). Despite its already high mileage, until it was withdrawn in 1930 RM 6 ran 80000 miles on the Cooktown. It was joined on the line in 1924 by the open sided RM 13 (RM 22 until 1929), a 40hp Studebaker with a capacity of 6, but less popular than RM 6 it was taken out of service late in 1932. The last four Rail Motors to serve the Cooktown were 45hp AEC type, having enclosed light metal bodies on the AEC 506 road chassis. The first to arrive was RM 32 *Endeavour* (RM 80 until 1929), and like the others which followed (RM 23, 25 and 58) had bodies 24ft 5in long overall, a four-wheel bogie at the front and a pair of 3ft diameter driving wheels at the rear. They had a centre buffer with link and pin coupling in order that they could haul up to two loaded wagons. After RM 32 had run 183,000 miles on the Cooktown, it was sent to QR Townsville in 1944 for overhaul before moving to the Normanton – Croydon line, where it remained in service until 1960. As the chapter heading indicates, in the painting the stalwart *Endeavour* is seen in 1937, taking the boiler of the Laura River dredger down to Cooktown. The Cooktown Railway was in many ways unique, even though not in its isolation, but surely must be the only one on which a train was derailed by an ant hill built across a rail in the interval between services.

The Cooktown Railway
J.W. Knowles, Australian Railway Historical Society (Queensland Division) 1966
Queensland Steam Locomotives 1900-1969, Design and Operation
J.W. Knowles, self published 2002
Railways of Australia
C.C. Singleton / D. Burke, Angus & Robertson 1963

CHAPTER TWENTY

1946 GULF, MOBILE & OHIO RAILROAD, USA
Ingalls Model 4-S B-B No. 1900 (Diesel-Electric)

The story of the devastation wrought on New Orleans by Hurricane Katrina in August 2005 has been told through the medium of innumerable images and through interviews with those who sadly were so affected, but almost ignored was that wrought on Pascagoula, lying to the east of the city and about 40 miles south-west of Mobile. 90% flooded by Katrina, its trials were largely unknown to the outside world, leaving its citizens justifiably aggrieved. Industrially, it is dominated by Ingalls Shipbuilding, founded in 1938 and suffering serious damage in the storm, but recovering to continue as a major builder of naval vessels and since 2011 a part of Huntington Ingalls Industries. Its attempt just after World War 2 to enter the diesel locomotive market and the railroad connections of the area constitute the focus of this chapter.

The history of the latter, indeed of all the lines northward from the Gulf of Mexico through Jackson to St. Louis and on to Chicago is long and complex, over the years, almost up to the present, one of frequently changing ownerships. This is not the place to attempt to unravel them all, sufficient to say that for our present purpose the story begins in 1917, with the formation of the Gulf, Mobile & Northern. This rose out of the remains of the bankrupt New Orleans, Mobile & Chicago, which had operated 370 miles of track between Mobile and Middleton, Tennessee, much of which was sub-standard and for over 50 miles without ballast. As a wartime measure, the US Government that December took control of the country's railroads, but because not strategically important, the NOM&C was left to make do and mend as best it could, with the inevitable result that by the end of hostilities it had become seriously run down. Afterward it fell into the hands of receivers, who, seeking someone to manage the operation until a 'better suited' individual could be appointed, unwittingly made an inspired choice, Isaac Burton Tigrett, a local short-line railroad president and 'small town banker.' He turned out to be a man of vision, instinctively able to select capable executives, turning a struggling railroad into a 2800 mile system extending from the Gulf to Chicago and from a junction at Roodhouse, north of St. Louis, west to Kansas City. Under his direction, lightly used passenger services were handed over in part to petrol-electric railcars and from 1932 also to a wholly owned bus company. Replacement of steam power was extended by the introduction of the Rebels, three trains formed of a streamlined leading-end diesel-electric power car having a 2'B wheel arrangement and 600hp 6-cylinder Alco 539 engine (it included mail and baggage compartments – a vehicle akin to today's British Class 43), followed by a buffet coach and a sleeper/observation coach. At busy periods a third coach was added between Jackson and New Orleans. Two sets, GM&N 352 and 353 were delivered in 1935 and the third, 354, in 1937, permitting the addition of a service between Mobile and Union, Mississippi, and bringing to an early end steam hauled purely passenger working on the GM&N. In 1938 the Southern agreed to sell to Tigrett a millstone round its neck, the Mobile & Ohio Railroad, and following Interstate Commerce Commission agreement, it and the GM&N came together as the Gulf, Mobile & Ohio. Tigrett's ambitions were not yet fulfilled, for although approaching the matter with caution, he had his eye on the Chicago & Alton Railway. This had the attraction of a first class route between Chicago and St Louis (where it met the new GM&O), but also included the highly unprofitable line west to Kansas City. The C&A had been purchased in 1931 by the Baltimore & Ohio, a decision which it bitterly regretted, and was no doubt relieved when in 1945 the GM&O took it off its hands. The latter had done so with the intention of selling on the Kansas City section to the Santa Fe and Burlington railroads, but as a result of protests made to the ICC by a number of other companies, it was thwarted in its aim. After World War 2 times remained difficult, the situation not helped by serious labour difficulties, cost-cutting was the order of the day and by the close of 1948 the sole surviving service on which passengers could travel behind steam was the Jackson - Dyersburg branch mixed. On 7 October 1949 the GM&O became an all diesel locomotive railroad. The remaining history of the company is one of mergers and de-mergers, including for a while indirect ownership by PepsiCo (via Illinois Central). Since February 1988 much of the surviving trackage has been in the hands of Canadian National, giving the company direct access to the Gulf of Mexico by way of the old GM&O route running due south from Chicago all the way to Jackson, where a fork to the left takes it to Mobile, right to New Orleans and Baton Rouge.

In 1943 the GM&O Board was advised by the Vice President, G.P. Brock, that full dieselisation would cost $9 million, but thereafter would save around $1 million annually, and even though the cost of initiating such a programme was raised considerably by the 1945 acquisition of the Alton, the company was not deterred and by the close of 1948 97% of main line freight and 75% of switching was diesel hauled. Trials with seven 1000hp diesel locomotives received during 1945 had been sufficiently successful for the company to place a firm order for 26; four 2000hp passenger, twenty 1500hp freight and two 1000hp switchers. GM&O diesels were to come from the established builders, Alco, transitioning from steam to diesel production under the Alco-GE banner, and Electro-Motive, a division of General Motors Corporation and in the business since 1935. A third, Baldwin, which never properly got to grips with the diesel era, was responsible for just two, GM&O numbers 280 and 281, Class 0-6-6-0 1000/2 NA10 and NA 11, maker's numbers 71580 and 71581, entering service on the GM&O at Jackson on 4 January and 12 February 1947 respectively.

Ingalls Shipbuilding, recognising that with the end of the War there would be a substantial reduction in ship orders, and observing that the growing market for diesel railway locomotives was creating a backlog of orders among the established makers, decided to have a go. It proposed a range of five different types, all utilising the marine diesel engines produced by Superior Engines & Compressors; they were 3-S, 1000hp, 4-S 1500hp, 5-S 1000hp, 16-S 660hp and 17A 2000hp. All were of B-B (UK Bo-Bo) wheel arrangement except 17A, which was A1A-A1A. Only one locomotive was constructed, the subject of this painting. Maker's number 1501, it was completed early in 1946 and photographed that March on the Ingalls slipways, dwarfed by the vessel alongside, bearing a simple unlettered work's livery, relieved only by a broad, light-coloured band along the bodyside. The specification was; 1650hp 660rpm V8 engine with 12½in by 15in cylinders, length overall 56½ft, width 10ft, weight in working order 32.7 tonnes (72000lb), fuel capacity 1000 US gallons, lubricating oil 150 US gallons and cooling water 280 US gallons. Capacity of the sand containers was 28ft³. There were many design features advanced for the time, not least amongst them the turret cab with rear vision, the top of the body casing inset to assist this. Even so, it was recognised there was a blind area close to the rear, and a low-level driving position was provided there for back-up and coupling purposes. On completion, Ingalls 1501 went out on trial to a number of railroads, including the Louisville & Nashville, Tennessee Coal & Iron, Seaboard Air Line and Southern. In June 1946 it was purchased by the GM&O for US$ 140,000, said in some quarters to have been only because the railroad wished to keep an important shipper happy, but even if there is some truth in that, the fact no customers appeared should not be taken as a reflection on the locomotive's performance. For twenty years, as GM&O No.1900, it worked all around the system, at different times out of Jackson, Mobile, Meridian, Laurel and finally, towards the end, Illinois. It was regarded as a freight locomotive, although it is known to have undertaken some passenger work, while the stylish early two-tone livery shown here was later downgraded to a plain unadorned red. Possibly Ingalls assisted with the provision of spares as necessary, but even so twenty years of service for a single non-standard locomotive is a good record. On withdrawal in 1966 it was traded-in to EMD, which recognising it was unique offered it to the Illinois Railroad Museum for US$3000, but the money could not be raised and in 1967 No.1900 was sold for scrap to the Pielet Brothers concern on the Indiana Harbour Belt. In the view of the author this was a most handsome machine. Of course this is a subjective assessment, but what cannot be disputed is that the Ingalls team got it right. Possibly that included individuals with railroad experience, taken on for the project, but even so this unique locomotive was a remarkable first effort. On the GM&O No. 1900 gained a fine reputation for the ruggedness of its construction, for its reliability and versatility. For these reasons, and the fact as a design it was ahead of its time, one can only regret that it has not survived.

Gulf, Mobile & Ohio, Color Pictorial
R.R.Wallin, FourWaysWest 1996

Diesel Locomotives, The First 50 Years
L.A. Marre, Kalmbach Publishing 1995

The Diesel Builders, Volume 3
J.F. Kirkland, Interurban Press 1994 (Baldwin Locomotive Works)

CHAPTER TWENTY ONE

1947 GREAT NORTHERN RAILWAY, IRELAND

McIntosh U Class 4-4-0 No. 205 *Down* 5ft 3in Gauge

The simple inside-cylinder passenger 4-4-0 was long a staple of British and Irish railway operation, for a hundred years from the second half of the 19th Century. As a type, it might be described as ordinary, unexceptional perhaps and its appearance in this volume on the face of it surprising. In fact, this particular example, Great Northern Railway U Class No.205 *Down* and its four classmates were remarkable, in that they were not constructed until as late in the steam age as 1947 and other than in detail were identical to five engines of 1915. All ten came from Beyer Peacock in Manchester, the second batch delivered in January 1948, works numbers 7244-7248, GNR 201 *Meath*, 202 *Louth*, 203 *Armagh*, 204 *Antrim* and 205 *Down*. In the same month Beyer Peacock also delivered five classic inside-cylinder 0-6-0s to the GNR, UG Class Nos. 145-149 and during August-September a further five 4-4-0 type, the three-cylinder VS Class, a modern express design with 6ft 7in driving wheels. Undoubtedly the final examples of their kind to be constructed, they had relatively short service lives, No.207 *Boyne* being the last to go in December 1965, outlived by the veterans of Austria (Chapter 5). The GNR engines were not the only examples of traditional design delivered across the Irish Sea by Beyer Peacock in later years. In January 1945 the Belfast & County Down Railway added to stock No.9, an inside-cylinder 4-4-2T identical to two sister engines of 1924, but it had a tragically short active life of only eight years, although not officially withdrawn until January 1956 (it had become Ulster Transport Authority

No.209 in 1950, the year in which the B&CDR was largely abandoned). One of Ireland's many minor lines, one of great charm and individuality, was the Sligo, Leitrim & Northern Counties Railway, which connected Enniskillen, on the GNR, to Carrignagat Junction, on the Coras Iompair Eireann line from Mullingar and Dublin. North from the junction the SL&NCR and CIE shared trackage to Ballysodare and Sligo. The company was famous for its family of inside-cylinder 0-6-4 tank engines, built in batches from 1882 and progressively enlarged, the final pair of 1949 being *Lough Melvin* and *Lough Erne* (running numbers were not used). As the SL&NCR, impecunious, was unable to pay, Beyer Peacock offered them to the GNR and UTA, then to two Australian systems of the same gauge, Victoria and South Australia, but without result. Finally, a hire purchase arrangement was made, the maker no doubt appreciating that suing the railway for breach of contract would be an unrewarding exercise, a £3000 deposit being paid (part Government funded), to be followed by payments of £500 per annum, ownership established by rectangular plates attached to the rear of their bunkers. That on *Lough Melvin* read, THIS LOCOMOTIVE MAKER'S No.7138 IS THE PROPERTY OF BEYER PEACOCK & Co Ltd GORTON, MANCHESTER, ENGLAND. The SL&NCR ceased running in September 1957, the closure of the GNR route through Enniskillen having deprived it of a vital connection, after which the two almost new 0-6-4T were first repossessed by the Manchester firm, then sold to the UTA in 1959, where they were numbered 26 and 27. The latter, *Lough Erne*, after withdrawal by Northern Ireland Railways in 1969 passed into preservation and currently is kept at the Whitehead depot of the Railway Preservation Society of Ireland.

In its earlier years the GNR did operate single-driver locomotives, 29 2-2-2 tender types inherited from predecessor companies and two 6ft 7in 4-2-2 of 1885, Class JS No.88 *Victoria* and No.89 *Albert* (Beyer Peacock 2519-2520). They were put to work on the Belfast – Dublin Limited Mail, a train of five six-wheel vehicles taking 3hr southbound and five minutes more north. As would be expected, loadings grew and in 1896 the pair were transferred to the Howth branch; withdrawal came in 1904. Otherwise, GNR passenger work was undertaken to the end by four-coupled types, tender and tank, assisted as required by several classes of 0-6-0 goods engine. Charles Clifford, who in 1895 succeeded James Park as GNR Mechanical Engineer, made enquiries of the Civil Engineer in March 1911 as to the possibility of building a 4-6-0, the latter's response taking the form of a diagram illustrating what he would allow. However, based on his maximum permitted axle load of 15 tons, the overall dimensions of the engine would have made it too long for the Dundalk Works traverser and too heavy for the erecting shop crane, difficulties which could have been overcome, but obviously involving an expenditure not considered worth while. Later, in 1929, the North British Locomotive Company in Glasgow was asked to estimate the cost of an outside-cylinder 2-6-2T as a substitute for the last five Class T2 4-4-2T (built by Beyer Peacock in 1929-1930), but the price quoted was considered too high.

The 1915 U Class engines essentially were a superheated tender derivation of the earlier T Class 4-4-2T, being usefully lighter, the T having a 16 ton 19 cwt axle load, the U 14 tons 14 cwt. This provided the latter with universal route availability over the GNR, indicated to operating staff by the presence of a white diamond mark on the end plate of the front buffer beam. Driving wheels were 5ft 9in diameter, two 18in by 24in inside cylinders with 8in piston valves were actuated by Stephenson link motion, working pressure was 175lb/in^2 and tractive effort 16763lb. The tender was GNR B Type of 2500 gallon water capacity. The second batch of 1947 differed in a number of respects. The cylinders were placed 2¾in closer and the boiler centre line 2½in higher at 8ft 2½in, while working pressure was the same at 175lb/in^2 (the boiler was pressed for 200lb/in^2). They were easily distinguished from the first group by having side window cabs and a new tender which looked a little like a scaled-down version of the standard Stanier LMS type. GNR Type D, they held 2500 gallons of water and 6 tons of coal, running on Hoffman roller bearing axleboxes. After World War 2, for steam locomotives designed and constructed on the British mainland for home use, the priorities were ease of maintenance and high availability, for which reason, in general, they were utilitarian in appearance, with as many working parts as possible visible and easy of access (an exception was Bulleid's double-ended Leader, which although it was intended to meet these criteria, in practice did not). On the face of it, the GNR's decision to buy more of the same may seem uninspired at the very least, but there was good reason. Much of the company's trackage ran through sparsely populated areas, with many long branch lines, high speeds were not required and loads generally light. The U Class 4-4-0s were good engines, capable of excellent running with loads of up to eight bogie carriages if required, but they did much of their work on the Dundalk to Omagh route and on the long branch which turned west at Bundoran Junction, running round the north side of Lower Lough Erne and terminating on Donegal Bay at Bundoran itself. The loads were normally two or three bogie coaches, with up to six vans at the rear carrying anything from bread to bullocks. L.H. Liddle (see sources) recalled being told by a GNR man "It's the tail of the train that pays on the Irish North." As after World War 2 only a small number of new locomotives were needed for what were undemanding duties, unlikely to become more onerous, the GNR's decision to order more of the competent U Class was common sense. They were thoroughly familiar to maintenance and operating staff. What was surprising in the austere early post-War years was the elaborate manner in which they were painted, a style reminiscent of the old Caledonian Railway. It was George B. Howden, who, following his appointment as Locomotive Engineeer in 1933, had introduced what is usually described as sky blue above the running plate, elaborately lined in black with white edging, and vermilion with white lining on bufferbeams, running plate valance and tender mainframes. Wheels had blue spokes and inner rims, with black centres outlined in white.

In the painting No. 205 awaits departure at Clones; just beyond, one of two railcars, C2 and C3, built at Dundalk in 1937. Having 102hp Gardner diesel engines, initially they ran as a pair, back to back, but were quickly separated, both working regularly out of Clones to Enniskillen. Clones at one time was an important rail centre, situated at the junction of the through route from Dundalk to Enniskillen and Omagh, of the line from Belfast via Portadown and Armagh, and of that from Cavan. Just visible also is the roof of the twelve road pre-cast concrete semi-roundhouse, designed by the Indented Bar Company of London and built in 1925. Another of identical design, long since demolished, was built for the GNR at Portadown, but this example still survives, though not having seen a locomotive since 1960 when the town's last rail links closed to goods traffic, three years after the end of passenger services. A remarkable and historically important structure of striking appearance, and of a kind unexpected in rural Ireland. Perhaps, though, even more remarkable to us today is the clutter of rodding and wires between the tracks, just at the right height to catch the shins of the unwary and, in poor light, positively dangerous.

Locomotives of the GNRI
N. Johnston, Colourpoint 1999

Sligo, Leitrim & Northern Counties Railway
N. Sprinks, Midland Publishing 2001

Steam Finale
L.H. Liddle, Irish Railway Record Society 1964

CHAPTER TWENTY TWO

1948 FC NATIONAL GENERAL BELGRANO, ARGENTINA
Porta 4-8-0 *Argentina* 1000mm Gauge

The formation of a nationalistic Argentine government in 1943 was followed three years later by the election as President of Juan Domingo Perón (1895-1974), a major consequence being the transfer to state ownership of foreign owned assets, the railways included. Their purchase cancelled a debt of £130 million owed by the British Government to Argentina at the close of World War 2 (although it should be noted not all railway companies had been British owned). Initially, the railways were constituted into six regions, that which interests us here being titled FC Nacional General Belgrano. This was made up of the metre gauge network totalling 14935 km, operated by the British-owned Central Córdoba, Midland and Transandino companies, by the French Santa Fe and Compania General, by the state's Central Northern and North Argentine and the local government of Buenos Aires' Provincial. At the same period, a young civil engineer, Livio Dante Porta (1922-2003), who from early childhood had been fascinated by steam locomotives, and who had become enthused by the work of André Chapelon in France (Chapter 35), with the self-assurance of youth made a direct approach to his new President, proposing a steam locomotive incorporating the latest technology and understanding of thermodynamics. He found a sympathetic ear in Perón, who made available to him the necessary funding via the Argentine national bank, albeit technically in the form of a loan. Accordingly, in 1948, the former Central Córdoba B22 Class 4-6-2 No.2011 was taken into the workshop Porta had established at Puerto de Rosario in Santa Fe province (on the Rio Paraná, about 300 km north-west of Buenos Aires). What re-emerged bore no resemblance to what had entered, and in reality all that remained of the former Pacific were some wheelsets and frame sections, together with the tender chassis.

The new locomotive was a four cylinder compound 4-8-0 (in the author's view, a consistently underrated wheel arrangement), internally very much in line with Chapelon's thinking, though with even more generous steam passages than advocated by him. The cylinders were inside 2xHP 360mm by 660mm and outside 2xLP 580mm by 560mm, with re-superheating between high and low pressure. A double Kylchap exhaust was provided. The all welded boiler worked at a pressure of 285lb/in², grate area was 3.9m² and coupled wheel diameter 1270mm. A deep, rocking grate was installed, with a large proportion of combustion air introduced above the fire. Wheel flanges were shallower than was usual, while the third coupled set had none, factors which apparently resulted in unusually smooth running and permitted speeds of up to 105km/h to be attained on what generally was poor quality track. The maximum axle loading was only 13.5 tonnes, while the weight of the locomotive in working order, not including tender, was 68 tonnes. Initial trials took place in and around Rosario, following which it moved south under its own steam to the former Buenos Aires Provincial system workshops at Gambier, La Plata, roughly 60km south-east of the capital. From there trial runs were made with freight trains, all of them loose coupled, the locomotive attaining 105km/h with a load of 1219 tonnes and 80km/h with 2032 tonnes. It proved able to produce 2100hp at the drawbar. Power to weight ratio matched the world's best at 31dbhp/tonne, and thermal efficiency achieved in practice was 11.9% (by comparison, the British Transport Commission report of October 1951 on types of motive power, their advantages and disadvantages, put the thermal efficiency of modern steam at no greater than 8% and for 'older' designs at 6%). Following exhibition on Roque Saenz Peña avenue in Buenos Aires, regular freight haulage was undertaken on lines to the south-west of the city until 1961, when it was withdrawn and stored in the open at La Plata. Finally, in the mid-1970s it moved back north, to Tucumán, eventually being placed on display, painted a dark grey overall, in the former North Argentine station there. By 2004 it had been moved into the closed running shed at Mate de Luna, where, covered in chalked graffiti it was gradually dismantled by thieves, destroying any hope of permanent preservation – even less of restoration to working order. A few years earlier Porta himself had planned not only to do so, but to incorporate also improvements gained from experience over half a century of work. One has to suggest that such a development would have been unlikely to revive the commercial fortunes of steam by then, but even so, as a conclusion to some truly inspired and eminently practical thinking, which has been built upon successfully by others – Day, Girdlestone, McMahon, Waller and Wardale, for example – the abuse suffered by the locomotive in its last years is nothing short of a tragedy.

It appears that Porta's 4-8-0 never carried a running number, being universally known as *Argentina*, a name carried on the front end of the framing for much of its career, although more correctly it ought to be referred to as *Presidente Perón*, for it was this title it carried on plates either side of the boiler until he left power in 1955. Additionally, the right-hand lower front body casing carried the words in Spanish, 'Better to do than to say' and the left 'Better to carry out than to promise.' It is not known whether or not Porta had a say in their choice, but they encapsulate his approach to his work rather well. Photographs of it at Rosario during construction and prior to painting shows the words Perón-Evita chalked on the casing, but the wife who perhaps has turned out to be the more enduringly famous of the couple was not included on the nameplates eventually applied. The final colour scheme was white overall, with trim in the Argentine national blue. Initially the smokebox was also white, but more practically this was later changed to black, as in the painting.

La Locomotive à Vapeur
A. Chapelon (English edition, G.W. Carpenter), Camden Miniature Steam Services 2000
The Red Devil and other Tales from the Age of Steam
D. Wardale, self-published 1998
World of South American Steam
R. Christian/K. Mills, Big Trees 1974
Author' own notes and observations and correspondence/conversation with Shaun McMahon. Also, here he breaks his rule and points the reader wishing full information on the sad tale of Argentina to Martyn Bane's thorough website: https://www.martynbane.co.uk/modernsteam/ldp/argentina/arg.htm

750mm gauge 2-10-2 No.107 (Mitsubishi 849/1956) at Rio Turbio, Patagonia, 15 December 2004. It carries the large Kylpor (Kylchap - Porta) exhaust as a visible reminder of the many improvements made to the coal railway's fleet of twenty, which revolutionised performance, but sadly by this time had either fallen into disuse or even been removed entirely. The headboard proclaims the planned tourist train service, which sadly seems unlikely now ever to materialise, a victim of political and industrial disputes. Here it is in decent condition generally, steamable, but with brake gear in serious need of attention. It carries the incorrect number 116, which locomotive at the same date was also at Rio Turbio. Present in open store were ten other examples, plus another nine in a compound at Rio Gallegos, at which location there was no longer any track.

Two further locomotives which have benefited greatly from Porta's work, in this case visibly in the form of a Lempor (Lemaître - Porta) exhaust, although many other improvements are incorporated. Both belong to the 500mm gauge Ferrocarril Austral Fueguino at Ushuaia, the 'Estacion del Fin del Mundo', starting point for the service which takes visitors to the Parque Nacional. At left is No.3 Camila, a 2-6-2T by Winson Engineering of Daventry (15/1995), upgraded in stages between March 1999 and October 2001. Behind is No.2 Ing. L.D.Porta, originally Nora, technically the first new steam locomotive constructed in Argentina (by Tranex, Carupa, 1994), but in view of the extent of the work carried out, perhaps Porto's Argentina might be considered an acceptable claimant for the title. No.2 is unusual for a Garratt in having the leading cylinders at the inner end of the power bogie, but as built was a scaled-down simple-expansion version of the first two Beyer-Garratts, compounds completed in 1909 for the 2ft gauge North East Dundas mineral tramway in Tasmania. The name was changed on completion of the upgrade on 11 December 2001 as a tribute to the man whose work had made such valuable improvements in performance possible. 17 December 2004.

CHAPTER TWENTY THREE

1953 EGYPTIAN STATE RAILWAYS, EGYPT
Jung B+B (Twin Unit Diesel Mechanical)

The first plan for a railway in Egypt was made as early as 1833, the brainchild of the country's then ruler, Mohammed Ali Pasha, who recognised the financial value to his country of providing a reliable connection between the Mediterranean at Alexandria and Suez on the Red Sea, lying as it did on the main route from western Europe and Britain to India. Rails and sleepers were ordered from England, arriving in Egypt in 1835, but as sufficient funds could not be raised the plan was abandoned and the rails were used three years later for an industrial tramway serving a quarry at Dikheila, intriguingly (for this early date) apparently steam operated. However, it was clear that with a regular and increasing flow of travellers passing between the two points a railway had become vital and in 1851 Egypt's new ruler, Abbas Pasha, signed a contract with Robert Stephenson for a standard gauge line from Alexandria, completed as far as Cairo in 1856. Initially the Nile at Kafr-el-Zayyat was crossed by pontoon ferry but two years after opening the heir to the throne, Prince Ahmed, was drowned when his train fell into the river, the result of which was the provision of a bridge with a turning span to permit the passage of river traffic. Onwards to Suez work was delayed, in part because agreement had been reached with France over the construction of a canal from Port Said on the Mediterranean to Suez, but the level of traffic was such that the coaches then used could no longer cope and the Cairo to Suez section opened in 1858. Until that time, between these two points, mail, baggage and general goods had gone by camel caravan, passengers in so-called vans. William Russell of The Times newspaper likened these to "Brighton bathing boxes placed longitudinally on wheels." He recorded that each van had four horses changed every eight miles, with stops at stations for meals. There was nothing visible "except sand, arid hills, camels (alive and dead) and vultures." Movement was largely at night when it was "quite cold." Unfortunately the Cairo to Suez railway in the opinion of some of its users turned out to be not much better, in their view quickly being allowed to become run down. A traveller wrote of it in 1863; "But such a train! Carriages of English make that had once been in order, now cracked with heat and neglect. Doors that would not open, bunches of horsehair sticking out of the cushions and looking less like vehicles for actual service than ancient relics. The railway itself came down to the beach in a casual way as though it were not quite sure whether it ought to be there." Maybe so, but these were early days of operating in extreme climatic conditions which must have been testing for those responsible for keeping things moving. One can imagine what it was like to be caught in a violent sandstorm accompanied by heavy rain, something which that same traveller experienced. When the seasonal Khamsin wind blew, sand built up over sleepers, platforms, roofs, working its way into the moving parts of locomotives and every nook and cranny of the carriages.

The Egyptian rail system expanded rapidly into the 1870s, but the strain placed on financial resources brought about a pronounced slowdown and it was almost a decade before there was a renewal. The difficulties had resulted in the formation of the three-man Council of Administration, with British (Chairman), French and Egyptian members, which retained control until 1905 (in this period the title Egyptian Government Railways was generally employed, Egyptian State Railways 1905-1954, Egyptian Republic Railways for a period thereafter and today Egyptian National Railways). The major trunk route south along the Nile from Cairo reached El Minya in 1870, Asyut in 1874, then Aswan via Luxor in 1892-1898. An extension from there to Sadd-El-Aali opened in 1968 (site of the Aswan High Dam). The long, lonely line along the Mediterranean coast from Alexandria via El Alamein today ends at Salúm on the Libyan border, the route beyond abandoned. A noteworthy addition to the network as recently as 1972 runs 350km south-west from Helwan into the Egyptian heartland to service the ore deposits at Bahariya. Cairo during World War 2 acted as headquarters for the allied Middle East Forces, bringing vastly increased traffic to the ESR; the official stock list in 1943 counted 594 steam and 22 diesel locomotives. At that time also there were a number of railcars, some diesel, but a surprising quantity of steam; the railway had received over the years 3 Hunslet (1912), 6 Clayton (1928), 18 Birmingham Railway Carriage & Wagon Co (1930) and 10 Sentinel (1935). The total is 37, but as the number in stock was 31, probably all three Hunslets had gone and perhaps three of the Claytons.

By early 1943 nineteen Whitcomb Bo-Bo diesel locomotives with two 325hp Buda engines (or 0-4-4-0DE as they were then described) were active on the Western Desert Extension. They burned oil, as did all steam locomotives on the ESR after the middle of that year, but had the added and significant advantage that they did not require regular replenishing with large quantities of water. The ESR also had ten active on the recently opened line from Qantara south along the east bank of the Suez Canal to El Shatt (opposite Suez itself). Most if not all the Western Desert Extension examples were moved to the Italian theatre in January 1944, but their performance had firmly established the advantage of diesel traction over steam. Soon after the war, in 1948, the ESR purchased twelve 1600hp 1A-Do-A1 diesel-electrics from English Electric and Vulcan Foundry, while others of varying arrangement rated up to 2600hp came over the ensuing years from such builders as Henschel, EMD and Voroshilovgrad. At the other end of the power range, 172 0-6-0DE (23) and 0-6-0DH (149) types arrived from 1948.

The build up of the armed forces in Germany during the 1930s led to a requirement for locomotives to work at munitions depots, airfields, storage tank farms and other military installations. To fulfil the need, a range of small diesel types was developed, rod-driven, having four, six or eight wheels. An office (Arbeitsgemeinschaft für Motorlokomotiven) was established at Wildau in June 1936 to co-ordinate design and development, the detail work allotted chiefly to Berliner Maschinenbau AG (former Schwartzkopff), but also to Orenstein & Koppel. Engines and drive systems were in the hands of Deutz and Voith respectively. BMAG was responsible for the most produced and best known variant, the type WR360C14, a 360hp 0-6-0 diesel-hydraulic (after 1945 DB type V36, later 236), construction undertaken by a number of firms. One, Jung of Kirchen-an-der-Sieg, had the honour, albeit sad, of delivering the last new steam locomotive to DB in December 1959, the 2-6-2 23 105. Jung's contribution to the WR360C14 programme was small, the firm being responsible for seven, works numbers 8505-8511 of 1939-1940. However, after the War the ESR placed an order for a modified version, having wheel diameter increased from 1100mm to 1232mm, improved cooling systems and other details under a taller external casing. Jung Type R361C, they were built for a maximum speed of 60km/h and to a 15.5 tonne axle loading; power supplied by 360hp MWM RHS 335S engines driving through Voith L37 hydraulic transmission, becoming ESR Nos.4211-4219 (Jung 11590-11598/1952) and 4220-4225 (11599-11604/ 1953). A second similar group, Jung Type R363C followed, ESR 4226-4246 (12161-12181/1955) and 4248-4252 (12182-12187/1956). They were largely employed on passenger work in and around Cairo, on which duty it appears they performed well. At the same time as the first order was placed, the ESR asked Jung for a more powerful version for freight work, specifically to haul heavy stone trains from the ancient gypsum quarries at Tourah, on the Helwan line immediately to the south of Cairo. The result was two twins, back to back, essentially the same as the 0-6-0 type, except that each had a full-width body and ran on four wheels, the drive to an intermediate crankshaft and providing for the pair 720hp. Jung Type R720B+B, works numbers 11586-11587 and 11588-11589 of 1952-1953, they were allotted ESR Nos.4401-4402, but never bore them as they were not accepted into stock. Accounts as to the reasons why vary. A Voith technician present on a trial run blamed poor track conditions at the quarries. The rails were often out of gauge and did not curve, simply changed direction at the joints. Even at very slow speed, the drive was damaged and one unit suffered a collapsed suspension. On the other hand, a later report stated that the two twins had constructional defects and as delivered were not properly in running order. The painting supposes an early trial, in which one of the two is heading south out of Bab el Luq station in Cairo towards Helwan. One final point; ESR (ENR) non-steam locomotives and railcars usually have vertical metal bars over the drivers' windows, but here they were not provided, prior to delivery at least. Perhaps, in the circumstances, they never were.

Jung-Lokomotiven Volumes 1 and 2
S. Lauscher/G. Moll, EK-Verlag 2012 and 2014

Middle East Railways
H. Hughes, Continental Railway Circle 1981

INTERLUDE

TRAMS
An Edinburgh Interlude

As the reader will be aware, the author is not immune to the steam or indeed other forms of tram, possibly because his home city of Edinburgh has employed more types of power than most, including the greatest use of cable haulage of any city other than San Francisco, the charm of the Scottish capital's variety exemplified by cable car No.51, about 1913. We know it is pictured in the Morningside district, as nowhere else in the world would a housewife call round to her local butcher to purchase a lamb shank for soup dressed in the latest Paris fashion (1).

San Francisco, of course, is in California, where in 1876 one S.R. Mathewson had proposed the rotary engine steam tram illustrated here (2) to the Edinburgh Street Tramways Company, which at the time was seeking an alternative to horse traction. It considered his idea, then rejected it; at that time probably it would not have appealed to Edinburgh's sense of what was fit and proper anyway. Much more seemly was electric tram No.35, seen in the 1950s on the long route out to Granton, crossing the swing bridge at Bernard Street in Leith (3). The livery was a splendid dark maroon and cream, appropriate to the city's image.

Of course, before the cable and electric trams, there had been horse trams, seen here in 1876 (4) from Register House at the top of Leith Street, looking west along Princes Street towards the Scott Monument and the Castle. This is based on an image by well known Edinburgh photographer Thomas Begbie. Most of his work, much of which featured old Edinburgh's ramshackle buildings and narrow cobbled streets, dates from the 1850s, making this a very late example and probably the only one to capture the tracks in place (service had commenced in 1871), although it has no trams in view.

The original system closed in November 1956, but in 2014 the first part of a new system, more modest in its planned extent, opened after considerable controversy. Now very successful, planning is under way for extension northward to the Leith and Newhaven waterfront, with bids being sought for two construction contracts, the decision whether or not to proceed due towards the end of 2018 (5 & 6).

A tram approaching the Gogarburn stop eastbound – Edinburgh Airport to York Place.

A tram approaching the Princes Street stop westbound – York Place to Edinburgh Airport.

Belgian Fancies; whoever suggested Belgium was dull? All the locomotives pictured here served the État Belge and for variety they take some beating, each of the four most prominent being unique in one respect or another.

Of the pair to the rear, the 2-2-2 at left is 'Le Dragon Belge', No.265. Built by Couillet in 1862 as a cab-forward 2-4-0, it was rebuilt to the form seen here by its maker in 1865, reboilered in 1881 and withdrawn in 1902.

At right is No.969, a double-Fairlie 0-6-6-0T by the Yorkshire Engine Company (212/1872), which was originally Grande Compagnie du Luxembourg No.108 Fenton (William Fenton at the time was GCL Board president). It worked freight on the Bruxelles-Namur line for a number of years, later locally around the capital, before withdrawal at Arlon in 1889.

Left foreground is No.761, an indirect-drive 0-6-0 by Carels Frères of Gand (Ghent), designed by Belpaire and Stévant. New in 1873, it was shown at Wien the same year, before taking up duty on heavy passenger trains between its home city and Bruxelles. It worked for just under thirty years, being withdrawn in 1901.

Finally, there is the distinctly exotic inside-cylinder double-barrel boiler 2-2-2T No.1452 of 1880, a product of the railway workshops at Malines (Mechelen), a cab-forward design for light, fast local passenger trains. Shown at the 1880 Bruxelles exposition, it bore a livery of bright bottle green, with cab and side tanks in pearl grey, lined in yellow. Although surviving until 1897, it was not successful and spent its entire life shunting within the works yard at Malines.

Behind No.761 is one of ninety-one Type 4 inside-cylinder, outside-frame 2-6-2T, built 1878 to 1882. This particular engine, No.1196, was exhibited alongside No.1452 in the purple livery shown, but was lost in the destruction and chaos of World War 1.

59

PART TWO

LOCOMOTIVES THAT WEREN'T

CHAPTER TWENTY FOUR

1856 HESSISCHE LUDWIGSBAHN, GERMANY
Maschinenfabrik Esslingen 4-2-0 (Crampton Type)

Among those present in the stuffy and dimly illuminated coroner's courtroom one late autumn day of 1862, as they awaited the return of the jury, there would have been mixed emotions. Sadness and a still sharp sense of loss for the relatives and colleagues of the deceased, apprehension perhaps for the representative of the London, Chatham & Dover Railway, and simple interest for the reporter from the Illustrated London News. He would have been pleased when his story appeared in full in that Saturday's edition, of 25 October 1862. It read; "The Coroner's jury in the case of Reed, the engine driver killed on the Chatham and Dover line, have returned a verdict of 'Accidental Death', adding their belief 'that the engine left the rails in consequence of the defective state of the road, which we consider mainly attributable to the use of engines known as Crampton's Patent'." The accident, readers were reminded, had taken place on Monday 13 October, when "for some unexplained cause the engine of the mail-train leaving Victoria Station at eight o'clock ran off the line as it was approaching a curve a couple of miles past Sittingbourne. After tearing up the rails for some short distance, it fell across the line. The engine driver was crushed to death, and the stoker and several passengers were severely, but not seriously, hurt." The jury's opinion reflected a common view of the Crampton, that it was inherently dangerous, but possibly the truth of the matter is that it was ahead of its time, in that track and roadbed were not yet ready for it. It never established itself in Britain, but later, in its most characteristic form with single driving axle to the rear of the firebox, did enjoy considerable success elsewhere, particularly in Germany and France, to the extent that in the latter country for many years one did not take 'le train', one took 'le Crampton.' The identity of the locomotive involved is unknown to the author. Perhaps it was not one of the LC&DR Cramptons, the type simply taking the blame, but equally it may have been such a locomotive, one of the five 4-2-0 of the Echo Class, then no more than eight months old and employed on the best Dover services. The leading carrying wheels were placed in a bogie, which having a central pivot and lacking side control did not take kindly to anything other than first-class track, and unfortunately at the time there was little of that on the LC&DR. Following an accident in 1861, the Board of Trade inspector had been scathing about the state of the company's permanent way, pointing to poorly packed ballast, broken chairs and lack of fish plates at joins.

Thomas Russell Crampton MICE MIMechE (1816-1888) was an original thinker par excellence, but with a tendency to be overwhelmed by the flow of his own ideas, resulting in many remaining unfulfilled. Equally, though, others did come to fruition, not just in the fields of locomotive design and general railway engineering. It is for the many innovative and often truly exotic locomotive designs that he is best known to the railway enthusiast fraternity. His introduction to railway engineering is widely considered to have taken place in 1839, when he joined the Broad Gauge Great Western Railway, working as an assistant under Daniel Gooch and being involved in the design of the successful Firefly Class 2-2-2, sixty-two examples of which were supplied 1840-1842 by seven different makers. This was not the case, as he had obtained previous, if limited, experience at the Cable Street foundry of John Hague (between Whitechapel and Stepney), where he served an apprenticeship from 1831 until he moved to Swindon. Hague, so far as is known, only built two railway locomotives, one a so-called 'common' 0-4-0, which may have been intended for the London & Greenwich Railway, but was purchased early in 1839 by the Stockton & Darlington. As *London*, later also numbered 42, it worked until around 1859. The other, one of the most original steam locomotives ever constructed, and also one of the most unsuccessful, was Lord Dundonald's rotary engine design of 1836 (see above right). One can imagine Crampton's fascination, and it seems possible that Lord Dundonald's obsession with achieving a low centre of gravity planted the seed which grew into what has become known as the classic stern-wheeler type, its purpose to combine speed with safety on the standard gauge. In 1848, he left the Great Western to set up on his own behalf as a Civil Engineer in London, although all but one of his six patents relating to improvements in steam locomotives were taken out before that date. Their variety was extraordinary and interested readers could do no better than refer to Mike Sharman's comprehensive book on the subject (see sources).

The view of the coroner's jury was not shared on the other side of the English Channel, where in contrast the stern-wheeler type, with outside cylinders and link motion, became well accepted. Behind its success lay not just steadiness in running, but also Crampton's advanced application of wide steam passages, large heating and generous bearing surfaces. The last of many French engines, the stately Paris – Strasbourg 210 (UK 4-2-0), No.80 *Le Continent* (Cail & Cie 189/ 1852), even survived World War 1 to be restored to working order at the C.F.de l'Est Epernay workshops in 1924 and today graces the national railway museum at Mulhouse. It was in Germany, however, that the classic Crampton was most widely operated, fifteen different companies owning a total of 135, all but one from indigenous makers in the years 1852 to 1878. The exception was Königliche Preussische Ostbahn No.35, Robert Stephenson 866/1852. One of the largest of the old independent railways was the Hessische Ludwigsbahn (HLB), opened between Mainz and Ludwigshafen in 1853, later becoming the major rail operator within the Grand Duchy of Rheinhessen and Starkenburg (in October 1897 it was incorporated into the Preussisch-Hessische Staatsbahnen). The HLB ran six 2A (UK 4-2-0) classic Cramptons, although latterly presenting a rather more austere appearance than was the norm, with replacement rimless chimneys and Charpentier brake equipment mounted on the right-hand footplating adjacent to the smokebox. The cylinders

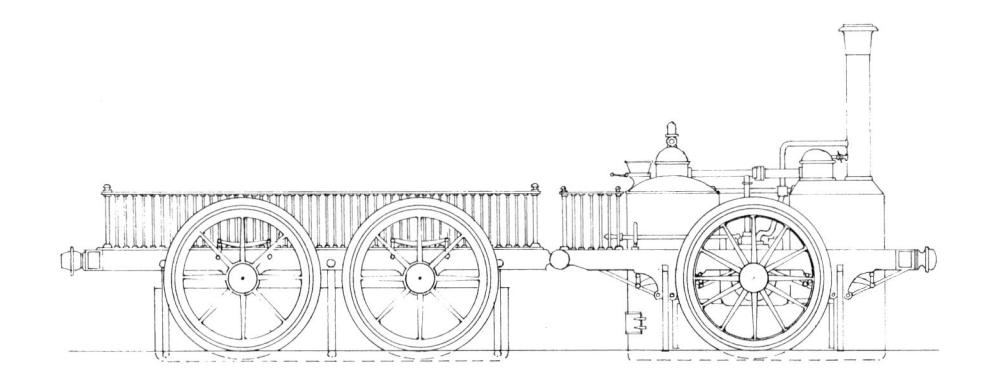

Crampton's first experience of locomotive engineering, Lord Dundonald's extraordinary rotary engine locomotive, the unique 0-2-0 built to his design by John Hague. As may be seen, its undersurfaces were intended to sit in a trough set between the rails, which coupled with outsize flanges to the wheels, and specially designed low centre of gravity carriages would permit safe operation on the elevated London & Greenwich Railway. It was completed and steamed, but almost certainly failed to move itself.

were 381mm by 610mm and driving wheels 1830mm diameter. All were built at Esslingen in 1858, works numbers 425-430, HLB 14-19, working all classes of train, chiefly between Frankfurt and Mannheim (works number 424, essentially identical, went to Denmark as Zealand Railway No.16 *H.C.Ørsted*, surviving until 1877, although it would seem seeing only intermittent use). The locomotive presented here is based on an Esslingen works drawing. Intended for the HLB, the company records confirm its function as 'Project No 2 einer Schnellzug-Locomotive für Mainz'. They give the leading dimensions in Imperial: 'cylinders 15" by 2' engl., driving wheels 6' engl., service weight 24 Tonn.' Dated 19 September 1856, the proposal is interesting in that the design is identical to the six Cramptons built two years later for the HLB, with one obvious difference. The latter had straightforward six-wheel tenders, but the earlier project, as may be seen, has a very basic two-wheel tender, attached to the locomotive with a simple drawbar, the faces of both footplates being convex to permit curving movements. One cannot imagine it affording a stable platform, especially in reverse running, although the arrangement at one time could be seen in Switzerland on a series of 0-6-2 tank engines, also Esslingen-built, which unlike this project, were not by any stretch of imagination 'express.'

The Crampton Locomotive
M. Sharman, self-published 1983

Emil Kessler 1813-1867
W. Distelbarth / J. Hotz (compilers) Deutsche Gesellschaft für Eisenbahngeschichte EV 1967 (Exhibition catalogue 100th Anniversary of death of Emil Kessler; Karlsuhe 1967)

Illustrated London News
25 October 1862.

BackTrack
November 1999/February 2000 (The 10th Earl of Dundonald, his Rotary Engine and his Locomotive Parts 1 and 2 Robin Barnes)

CHAPTER TWENTY FIVE

1874 HURD & SIMPSON, UK
0-6-0WT (Underground Locomotive)

The useful web publication Grace's Guide informs us that the Wakefield firm of Hurd & Simpson, makers of mining machinery, in February 1876 had entered proceedings for liquidation. These had been instituted by Frederick Hurd, of Wood Street, Wakefield, Yorkshire, mining and mechanical engineer, 'formerly carrying on business with Edward Thornhill Simpson of Walton, in the said county, Soap Manufacturer and Colliery Owner.' Also involved had been Charles Henry Simpson, possibly a brother of the latter. The business appears to have retitled itself and its activities more than once, but our present interest concerns the period during which it functioned as Hurd & Simpson's Patent Mining Machine Company. It was certainly involved with coal cutting machinery by the late 1860s, but 1874 seems to have been the peak year for promoting its products, two of which were rail mounted self-propelled two-cylinder four-coupled compressed air coal cutters, one for working at facings 4ft 6in in height, the other for 2ft. Also advertised that year was the subject of this chapter, 'Hurd and Simpson's Patent Locomotive Engine.' It is possible to see that in these the company's ambitions had over-reached its resources, leading to the bankruptcy proceedings which took place in the County Court of Yorkshire, in Wakefield. The official announcement was promulgated on 20 February 1876: 'Notice is hereby given, that a First General Meeting of the creditors of the above-named person has been summoned to be held at the office of Messrs Harrison & Smith, Solicitors, in Chancery-lane, Wakefield aforesaid on the 15th day of March 1876 at three o'clock in the afternoon precisely.'

The locomotive was subject to a patent application dated 31 July 1873, entered by Hurd and Simpson, for a 'new motive power generator.' The Engineer, issue of 21 August 1874, printed an engraving of the locomotive, partly sectioned to show interior details, and a brief description. The products of combustion from the firebox were to be returned to it by means of an injector 'actuated by compressed air or other equivalent agent.' In other words, the exhaust fumes from the coal fire were to be forced back into it, in a closed circuit, although compressed air or 'other flammable fluid or liquid' could be added if desired. The firebox, or 'fire receptacle', located immediately beneath the hopper was automatically fed by screw and shovel, worked by an arm connected to the beam close to its upper end. Air pumps adjacent to the boiler drove on to the upper end of the beam, which imparted motion through a rearward extension of the coupling rods. Steam 'combined with the highly heated and expanded gases' was led to the cylinders, or 'back again into the boiler when the engines are not working.' There would thus be no exhaust to atmosphere, permitting it to be safely employed under ground. The Engineer advised that the locomotive was nearly ready for trial, but restricted itself to the cautious comment that if the invention could be made to work, then substantial savings in fuel might be expected.

As a correspondent to the Industrial Railway Record remarked in 1971 (see sources), "a better way of killing the fire would be hard to imagine, short of pouring water on it." The provision of a dome-mounted safety valve in this instance one might consider an extravagance. It should be noted that the designers intended the locomotive to run cab forward, which presumably is the reason why sand is led only to the leading edge of the centre coupled wheels. Setting aside for the moment the sheer impossibility of getting the locomotive to work, it is pertinent to ask what the promoters had in mind. As mining engineers, familiar with the industry, they would have been fully aware that for any machine, in particular a locomotive, to work underground it would have to be of limited dimensions. Obviously, if working in and out of mine shafts, such a locomotive could only operate cab forward in one direction. Not only is this designed for standard gauge, it is too generously proportioned for ordinary underground mine workings. It is clear some effort was made to provide an attractive appearance, at least at the front end – the rear has definite limitations – and a fully lined livery style is suggested. Perhaps the projectors were being truly ambitious, hoping to break out, as it were, from the confines of mine railways to the main line. By 1873 the underground system in London had been in operation for a decade, the Metropolitan line from 1863 and Circle more recently, running their trains with steam locomotives which, designed to consume their own smoke, manifestly failed to do so. In the stations globe gas lights showed dimly through the drifting clouds of steam, sooty droplets and sulphurous fumes. The American writer Elizabeth Robins Pennell wrote that "the foreigner, eager to know from the beginning the worst that can be, has only to make his first descent at Baker Steet, Gower Street, or Portland Road. Ten chances to one he will never have courage for a second." Some were less concerned, even taking a positive view, certain physicians being known to advise patients suffering from respiratory disorders that a trip underground would work wonders on congested bronchial tubes. There were other sections of railway running underground, in the form of extended tunnels, operated by supposedly condensing and even non-condensing steam locomotives, where one which could genuinely and efficiently consume its own exhaust would find a welcome, but Hurd & Simpson's creation was not it. It is difficult to know whether or not it was constructed. The Engineer article implied that it was, but one wonders. It seems unlikely the company would have had the ability and facilities to assemble such a railway locomotive itself.

It is interesting and surprising that straightforward coal burning non-condensing steam locomotives, albeit of small dimensions, were constructed and operated underground, but in general not for extended periods of time. In this country, for example, to the design of George Eustace, Bickle & Company of Plymouth completed a tiny 0-2-2 saddle tank designed to work in the 278 fathom level (1668ft/508.4m) of the Levant tin and copper mine in Cornwall. The poor track and steep grades proved too much, while years later a former employee recalled that when the engine was working, visibility in the mine was nil. Delivered in April 1892, five months later it had returned to the surface, replaced by a pony. Two 19in gauge 0-4-0 tank engines that did have lengthy careers on such work, just over half a century, were *Ant* and *Bee* (Stephen Lewin, Poole 684-685/1877), which served the lead mine at Great Laxey on the Isle of Man until closure in 1929. They were cut up in 1935, but happily have been reincarnated in the form of working replicas built in 2004, which instead of tubs of ore haul visitors to the present day heritage centre. An interesting variation on the theme of exhaust diversion was to be found in a 750mm gauge 0-4-0WT built by Jung (69/1889) for 'Zentralbahn Basel'. At first sight absolutely standard, close inspection would have revealed a condenser beneath the footplate (for steam exhaust) and a tank between the frames ahead of the smokebox containing 'kalkmilch' (presumably a powdered limestone/water mix), into which the products of coal-fired combustion were diverted in tunnels, the greater part of the chimney being folded down to the right and the blastpipe capped. It worked for a number of Swiss concerns until 1938.

This interpretation one can imagine as a contemporary Punch cartoon, with the kind of caption then obligatory:
Street sweeper (hopeful; doesn't much like horses):- **"Pull a good load, will it?"**
Driver (morose; had planned to spend Saturday afternoon watching the home game):- **"Have to move itself first."**

The exhaust steam emitted by the fireless locomotive could cause discomfort and obscure vision in confined locations, but it was not flammable or noxious, and dispersed rapidly. Of the 90 examples built by Hannoversche Maschinenbau-Aktiengesellschaft of Hannover-Linden between 1884 and 1931, a number were intended for use underground. One was this neat 600mm gauge 0-4-0 (10375/1924) with driving positions at either end, built for the Oberpfalzewerke, Ponholz (about 20km north of Regensburg, Bavaria).

Industrial Railway Record
No.38 August 1971, Reader's letter with editorial additions (also Grace's Guide web page)

The London Underground
A. Emmerson, Shire Publications 2010

Feurlose Lokomotiven
K. Pokschewinski, Lokrundschau Verlag 2000.

CHAPTER TWENTY SIX

1889 MALLET-BRUNNER, GERMANY
2-4-2 (Two-Cylinder Compound)

Locomotive à grande vitesse système Mallet-Brunner

J. A. MAFFEI   MUNICH   BAVIÈRE

This chapter does not involve itself with the discussion which continues to this day over the advantages or otherwise of compound expansion in steam railway locomotives; that is, the use of steam in more than one stage. In compounding, after being exhausted from the cylinder at a pressure at which it is still capable of doing useful work, instead of passing wastefully to atmosphere, it is passed to a second, larger cylinder at lower pressure and then exhausted externally. In practice, it was applied to locomotives having two, three and four cylinders (the latter variety has been noticed in Chapter 7). The Erie Triplex (Chapter 12) had six of the same dimensions, a compound only of necessity and therefore uncharacteristic. Here, sides are not taken, because there are well-founded arguments for and against and the author does not consider himself competent to form a considered judgement – although, if pressed, he will say that what he would like to have seen on Britain's railways was a medium axle-load three-cylinder simple 4-8-0 with 5ft 8in (1727mm) drivers, light-oil fired, incorporating a thoroughly scientific approach to all aspects of its design, not streamlined and not overly exotic in external appearance.

The first tentative applications of compound expansion to railway locomotives were made about the middle of the 19th Century. As an early example one might propose the 6ft gauge Erie No.122, originally completed as a two-cylinder simple by the Boston Locomotive Works in 1851, but rebuilt by the railroad to John Lay's Patent in 1867. The original 26in piston stroke was retained, but new 11½in high pressure cylinders were placed ahead of the 24in low pressure on each side, each pair sharing a common piston rod. Interestingly, in 1885 the North British Railway did the same with No. 224, a Wheatley 4-4-0 of 1871, retaining the original 24in stroke, the HP cylinders 13in diameter and LP 30in. Not a success, it was returned to its two-cylinder simple form two years later. What really set compounding on

If all this were not sufficiently unusual, it will be seen from the plan view that the valve gear is fixed asymmetrically, on the left hand side of the locomotive, the forward and reverse eccentric rods reaching back to the expansion link beneath the cab, from where the valve rod passes forward beneath the trailing coupled axle to the valve chest attached below the high-pressure cylinder. The low pressure valve chest is on top of the cylinder, but its valve rod is not shown on diagrams; also the exact type of valve gear is not identified. It will be seen from the painting that a wide firebox is provided, but what is not evident is that in order to remain clear of the valve gear, it is extremely shallow and extends deep into the cab, resulting in cramped footplate conditions. Not evident too is that the axle boxes of the two rear sets of wheels permit radial movement. Simple or compound working could be selected, as desired. The leading dimensions were given as follows: cylinders stroke 610mm, diameter HP 530mm, LP 790mm; working pressure 11.57atm (170lb/in²); grate area 2.25m²; total heating surface 160m²; driving wheel diameter 2000mm; height rail to boiler centre line 2500mm. Two prominent railway engineers were behind this truly remarkable proposal, Anatole Mallet and his friend, A. Brunner, then chief engineer at J. A. Maffei of München. It originated with Mallet, who in order to avoid the complexity of three or four cylinders in rigid frame locomotives, and the shouldering caused by two outside cylinders, aligned them between the frames, creating a two cylinder compound able to run smoothly at high speed (the intended rate was not specified). Would the firm of Maffei have been prepared to take on and market such a design? It is most unlikely, but here artistic licence has permitted it to be aimed at the French and Belgian markets.

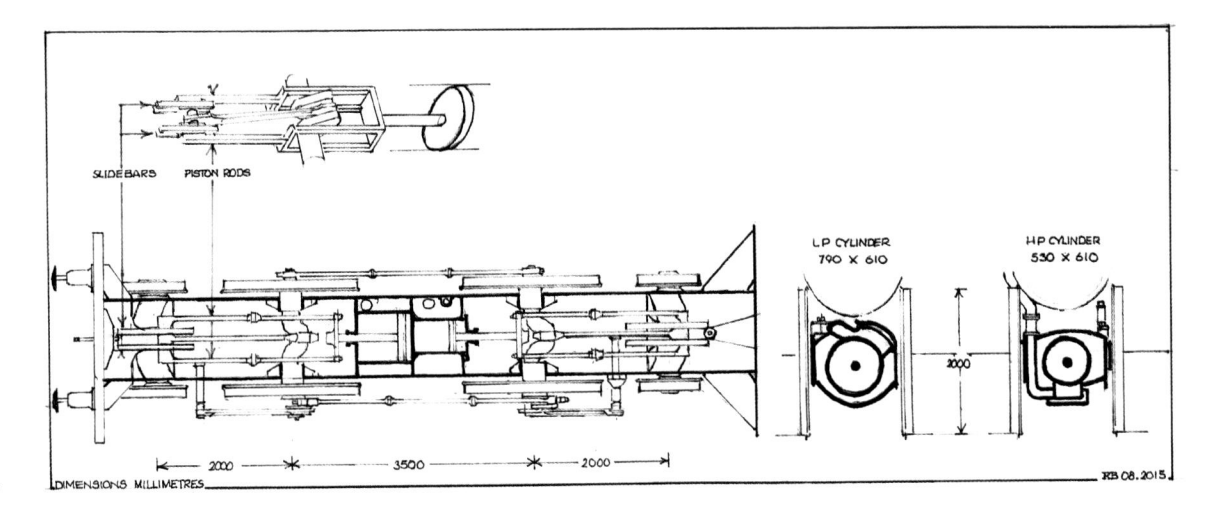

---

the move was Anatole Mallet's two-cylinder 0-4-2T, three of which were constructed by Schneider of le Creusot in 1876 for the Bayonne to Biarritz railway. Attractive little machines, weighing 20 tons, in which for purely cosmetic reasons the high pressure cylinders had false outer casings to match those of the larger low pressure. They sported very tall chimneys made necessary by double-deck carriages and proved most successful, establishing a vogue for the compound with two outside cylinders which lasted for more than half a century. This was not so in Britain, though with the two cylinders set between the frames it did enjoy success on the North Eastern Railway, both in express passenger and slow goods service. Excellent examples were two classes of 4-2-2, I with 7ft 1¼in drivers, cylinders stroke 24in, diameter HP 18in and LP 26in and J with 7ft 7¼in drivers, cylinders stroke 24in, diameter HP 20in and LP 28in. There were ten of each, built by the NER at Gateshead 1888-1890, their main duty being the lightweight business expresses between Leeds, Bridlington and Scarborough, on which, hauling perhaps 90 tons, they were known to attain speeds of 85mph. On one occasion, during which indicator diagrams were being kept, hauling eighteen four-wheel carriages one of the engines developed 1069hp on level track. They were the only Singles to have Joy valve gear, in a somewhat awkward and fragile arrangement in which the valve drive was taken by shafts and pendulum levers from inside the frames to the steam chests, which were located outside. This may have been one reason why, although their running could be very fine, all were converted to simple expansion with Stephenson valve gear between 1894 and 1902. In all, at one time the NER had over 250 compounds with two inside cylinders, of 4-2-2, 2-4-0, 4-4-0, 0-6-0 and 0-6-2T wheel arrangements, plus little *Aerolite* of 1869 which survives today in the National Collection in its final 2-2-4T form. One argument in favour of inside cylinders, compound or simple, is that with both as close as possible to the locomotive's centre line, the shouldering action produced by piston thrusts is greatly reduced (and see also Chapter 34). Elsewhere in the world, in particular where British influence at best was indirect, the view tended to be otherwise, both designers and operators preferring to have cylinders accessibly mounted outside the frames, although often with valve gear inside. But, as always, there were exceptions. In Germany, the Pfalzbahn (Palatinate Railway; incorporated into the Royal Bavarian State Railways in January 1909) had twelve inside cylinder simple expansion, part double-frame 4-4-2s, Class P3[1], built by Krauss of München 1898-1904. They were acquired specifically for the type's 'quiet and easy' running qualities, although as early as 1913 they were extensively rebuilt as four cylinder compounds. The Baden state system had 35 neat inside cylinder simple expansion 4-4-0s by three different builders 1892-1900, which would not have looked out of place here in Britain, while the Main-Neckar ran 15 double-frame inside-cylinder 2-4-2s built by Cockerill (1892) and MGB Karlsuhe (1902). Later Prussian Type S2, to German eyes these would have been most unusual locomotives, essentially Belpaire's État Belge Type 12, but with a narrow firebox, enlarged cab and two-bogie tender.

The project pictured shared with the Main-Neckar locomotives the wheel arrangement and inside cylinders, but the resemblance was no more than superficial, for internally it was very different, probably unique. When he first learned of it, the author regarded it as a tandem compound, but it was not, for although the high and low pressure cylinders sat horizontally in a line, they did not share the necessary common piston rod. The accompanying diagram demonstrates this. Both cylinders were located between the driving axles, which were spaced at 3500mm, the low pressure cylinder driving forward and high pressure to the rear. The length of the coupling rods was not considered to present a problem. The driving axle cranks were set at 90° to avoid a dead centre position, the diagrams also indicating the disposition of piston rods and slidebars.

Locomotive Compounding And Superheating, etc.
J. F. Gairns, Charles Griffin 1907

Compound Locomotives
J. T. van Riemsdijk, Atlantic Transport Publishers 1994

The author is indebted to Patrick Jacobs in Germany, who first drew the project to his attention and subsequently provided both the information and the drawings which enabled him to prepare these images.

CHAPTER TWENTY SEVEN

1894 CHASE-KIRCHNER, USA
Aerodromic System c11ft Gauge

Overhead railways have appeared in a number of forms, conventional, in which two rails, usually of standard gauge, have been employed, the monorail (frequently a mis-identification, additional guide rails often being provided) and most recently the Maglev ultra high speed type, which of course does not require a rail, or rails, of the traditional kind. Conventional overhead railways have been frequently found in heavily congested urban areas, and one thinks of New York and Liverpool as examples. The monorail type generally has struggled, although a long term survivor is Carl Eugen Langen's suspended type 13.3km line along the narrow valley of the river Wupper in Germany. Opened in 1901 it still performs its original function, offering genuine public transportation to the inhabitants of Elberfeld and Barmen.

There have been over the years a multitude of projects, some completed, such as in Sydney, but ultimately mostly unsustainable, though that in Seattle survives and is now designated as being of historical importance. Additionally, São Paulo in Brazil has an expanding system equipped by Bombardier. The Maglev has found the going hard and not established itself except in China (possibly it may do in Japan), where it cannot be described as providing public transportation in the commonly accepted sense. Apart from the expense of construction and maintenance, there are objections to elevated railways of any kind across open country, one the difficulty of detraining passengers in the event of a mechanical or other problem. More subjective is the argument that they are visually intrusive.

This elevated system was intended not simply to reach into open countryside, but to cross vast distances, where centres of habitation might be few and far between. The projectors, G. N. Chase, a US Army lieutenant, and H.W. Kirchner, described their plans in a 60 page booklet published February 1894 in St Louis, Missouri. They divided their arguments into The Present System, An Ideal System and the Aerodromic System, this last followed by a detailed description. In appendices were nine sets of diagrams and tabulated calculations. The first argument was an extended discussion of the present day (1893) railroad system in the United States. Managers were under increasing pressure to provide ever-faster services and forthcoming advances in rolling stock and track quality, it was said, would soon allow of an average speed of 60mph between cities. However, Chase and Kirchner argued, there were two conditions "necessary to make the present system perfect" that could never be met; the abolition of grades and of curves. There was a solution to be found in radically different construction. It might not be possible to dispense with grades, but possible to render them inoperative as obstacles to high speed. Very substantial savings were to be made through the elimination of curves (by reduction in rolling resistance), while considerable unnecessary cost was being incurred through the haulage of what the authors described as "non-paying tonnage." Here they quoted figures. For example, in the USA, in 1890, the average number of passengers per train was just 41, less than the capacity of a single coach, and the average freight haul, per train, was 180 tons, or 10 tons per loaded car. A report produced by the Lake Shore & Michigan Southern Railroad demonstrated that for every passenger carried in a Pullman car, empty weight 40-50 tons, 5 tons of non-revenue weight was transported. In Great Britain, "where the cost of roads and equipment is three times greater than in the United States, less than 5% of the total weight of passenger trains and only about 30% of the freight trains" is remunerative, or "less than 17% of the total tonnage." Concluding this part of their case, the projectors pointed out that as freight and lesser trains had to wait in loops to allow the passage of crack expresses, their crews often were idle "one-fourth of the time."

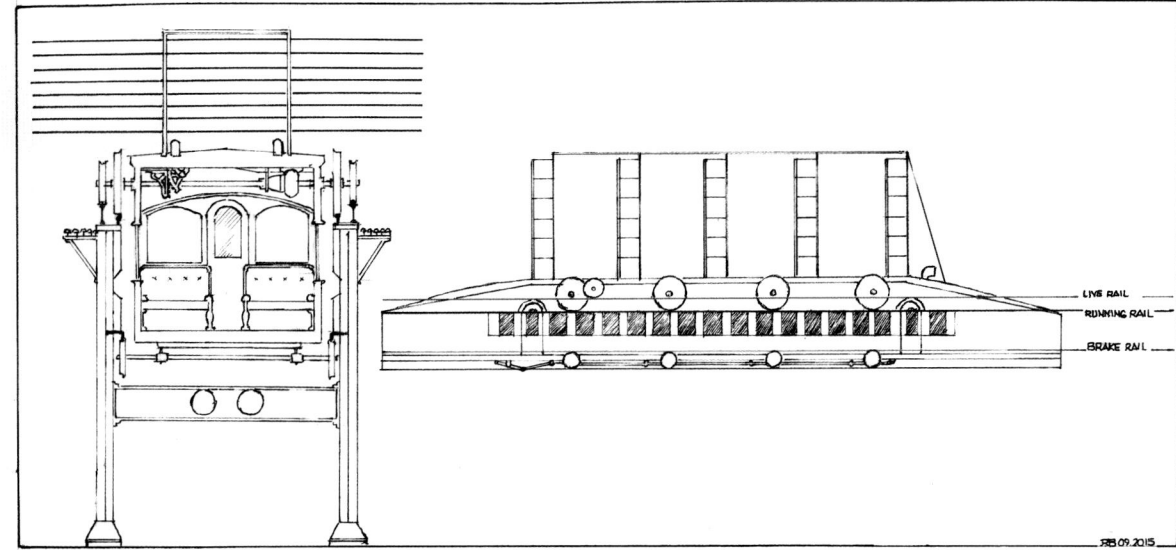

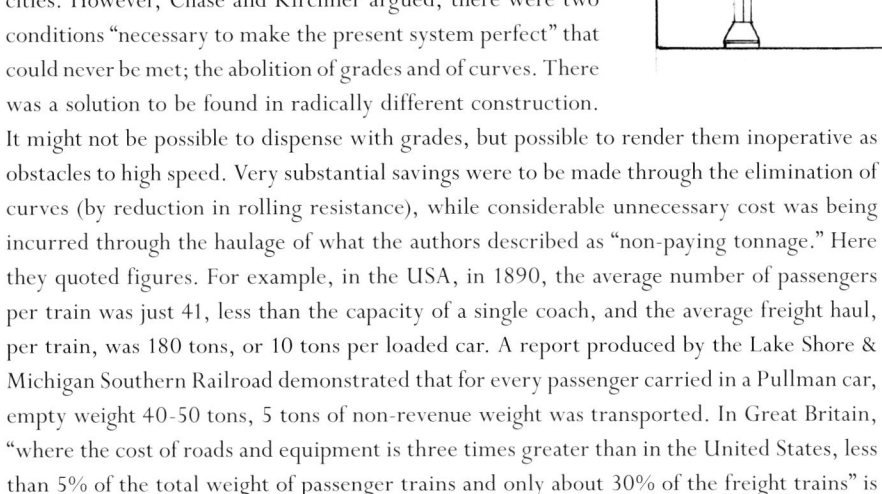

In the book's second section, its authors accepted that "aerial navigation" would be "the very acme of rapid transit," but were of the view that its realisation would be not be achieved within the foreseeable future. The two main obstacles were the difficulty of controlling the machine and providing sufficient power "to propel it any considerable distance." They had in mind the steam engine, which eventually was developed sufficiently for use in aircraft (Chapter 32). Thus they concluded that by "omitting several of the conditions" relating to aerial navigation, a commercially viable system could be evolved, "vastly superior" to the present one (the conventional railroad). The Aerodromic System of Transportation was a compromise between rail and air; in the case of the former it eliminated the obstacles to greater speed, namely grades, level crossings and curves, and of the latter the problems associated with safely controlled flight. There then followed a lengthy discussion of the experiments undertaken by Professor Samuel Langley into heavier than air powered flight, before finally the authors arrived at a "General Description of the Aerodromic System." Electric power would be supplied from stations located as convenient, but "for long distances it will not be necessary to burn a pound of fuel," for the "water power of every stream crossed can be utilised by turbine wheels" and, of course, "the same water can be used over and over again." Pick-up by the single unit vehicles was by wheel running on two live rails atop the structure located outside the running rails (in red on the side elevation above right). An advanced feature, proposed a decade ahead of the New Haven's pioneering installation (Chapter 14), was to be the use of alternating current. The authors stated that recent "actual" use of alternating current had demonstrated an efficiency of 76% over 108 miles, "or a maximum distance between power stations of 216 miles", against 28 miles for direct current. The general appearance of the structure may be seen from the accompanying illustrations, and while the diagrams in the book were not scaled, we know that the rails were "about 11ft apart." The support columns, normally spaced at 37ft, were set in stone and extensively braced. Curves might be introduced in the vicinity of stations, but otherwise the track would follow a direct line, which would mean that at 125mph the traveller from New York would "reach San Francisco inside of 24 hours." Furthermore, "at this speed the fruits of California could be placed upon Eastern tables with their bloom unsullied, and flowers with the dew still upon them." This could all be achieved through motors "of a type yet to be chosen" taking current at 5000V to 10000V, converted to 500V for the motors, but the crucial provision was the wings, "aeroplanes", fixed to masts atop the car body, in groups of three or four according to the specification of the car (these could be of different lengths between 40 and 100 feet, dependent on function. Passenger cars would be electrically heated and lit, while as the windows were fixed, they would be ventilated "through tubes, with automatic valves"). The planes, 20-30ft long by 4-5ft wide, again dependent on the size of the car, would have a lifting surface of 2000-4000ft^2, with the angle of attack of the leading edge adjustable between neutral and +10° or more. The idea was that on an upgrade the lift provided by the planes would negate the additional resistance, while on a downgrade, by maximising their angle, the engineer could create a braking effect which would complement the mechanical system, actuated by compressed air and working on the green rail in the diagram. Scams aimed at gullible investors were common at the time, but on the face of things this was not one. If it was, ten out of ten to Chase and Kirchner for effort. As to the painting, the intention was to depict a car speeding across the arid mid-West. It appears, though, to be crossing the surface of another planet, which on reflection might be considered a more appropriate location.

The Coming Railroad. The Chase-Kirchner Aerodromic System of Transportation
G.N. Chase / H.W. Kirchner, St Louis, Missouri 1894 (the author's copy is a Nabu Public Domain Reprint)

CHAPTER TWENTY EIGHT

1918 LANCASHIRE & YORKSHIRE AND CALEDONIAN RAILWAYS, UK

Hughes (L&YR) 2-10-0 and Pickersgill (CR) 2-10-2

Summer weather in Scotland has always been variable, and although at Carstairs station on 4 July 1960 it was grey with occasional wind-blown showers, it was no more than typical. In truth, in the author's recollection, Carstairs was always windy, but that was hardly a deterrent to the train watcher as even at that date the working was still almost exclusively steam powered. What did make the day a little different, and why it is remembered particularly, was an old Caledonian Pickersgill 4-4-0, BR 54505, pottering around the station area with a short train of low sided wagons and a brake van. A small group of permanent way staff were engaged in shovelling spoil on to the train, which at one point stopped on the through line parallel to the down side of the station platform. When the driver opened the regulator to move forward, the guard at the rear must still have had his brake on, for the couplings pulled taut from both ends of the train with a loud clang and the author watched astonished as the wagon in front of him momentarily was lifted clear of the rails. The reason was the wagons had non-adjustable three link couplings, while the train was not continuously braked from the locomotive. Even after the end of steam in Britain, for a time in some areas the replacement diesel locomotives were required to haul unfitted trains, and as had always been the case, great skill was required from driver at one end and guard at the other to prevent excessive snatching of couplings and sometimes consequential breakages. Most British goods trains trundled along at painfully slow speeds, one of a number of reasons why as competitive forms of transport developed they made such massive inroads into an activity which once the railway had dominated. What it did mean also is that there was only a limited need in this country for the kind of powerful freight locomotive to be found no great distance away in continental Europe, where continuous brakes were earlier adopted (even light freight and shunting locomotives, tender and tank, often were so equipped). There were exceptions, of course, because as competition grew, a number of tightly timed fitted freights were introduced, but largely the picture remained as described.

The dominant British goods locomotive of the steam age was the inside-cylinder 0-6-0 (Chapter 34), some of which were vacuum or air-brake fitted, but only in order that they could on occasion haul passenger stock. The most striking illustration of the reluctance to modernise was the 33 strong class of Beyer Garratt locomotives on the LMS, in which only the first three were train brake and screw coupling fitted, the remainder having just the archaic three link coupling. Beyer Peacock, forced to build them to a LMS Derby specification, must have been deeply disheartened, when the fleet could have served as a showcase for what fundamentally was a sound and versatile design. It was not until 1944 that the ten-coupled freight locomotive entered regular service in Britain, in the shape of the War Department 2-10-0. Air-braked, 150 were built over 1943 and 1944 for service overseas, some going initially on loan to the LNER and LMS, but by the end of the latter year all had moved abroad, 103 to Belgium and Holland, others to Egypt. From there a number later moved on to Syria and Greece, where they had lengthy working lives. The British Transport Commission purchased 25 in 1948, BR 90750 to 90774, which now vacuum fitted, were allocated to Scottish Region sheds at Grangemouth, Motherwell, Carstairs and Carlisle Kingmoor, from within which group they remained until withdrawn in 1961-1962. That same July day in 1960 at Carstairs, two of the class made an appearance, 90750 passing through on a southbound freight, which at least had a group of fitted vehicles at the front, and 90753 which arrived light engine in company with another Caledonian stalwart, Pickersgill 0-6-0 BR 57670.

The WD and BR 9F engines of 1954 may have been the only examples of the 2-10-0 wheel arrangement to operate in Britain, but they were not by any means the first projected. The even more substantial 2-10-2 had been proposed also, thirty years before the appearance of the WD engines. The Great Central Railway moved a heavy coal traffic from the Yorkshire mines to the company docks at Immingham, the flow of which was eased following the opening just before World War 1 of the Doncaster avoiding line. Its General Manager, the recently knighted Sam Fay, who amongst many other aspects of railway operation took a progressive view of freight train operation, wished to move the coal from the new concentration yard at Wath to the docks in rakes of 100 specially constructed 40-ton capacity wagons. During a visit to the USA in 1913, accompanied by senior officers, including the Locomotive Superintendent J.G. Robinson, the provision of suitable motive power was discussed with the Baldwin Locomotive Works at Philadelphia. Whether or not the builder was asked to do so, or it was on its own initiative, is not known, but the following year it outlined a large 2-10-2. Four cylinders 18in by 30in were indicated, driving 4ft 8in diameter coupled wheels. Working pressure was 190lb/in^2 and grate area, hand fired, 57ft^2. Adhesive weight was 100 tons, all up weight 121 tons. Tractive effort at 85% boiler pressure was 56100lb. The bogie tender was very much in the North American style; capacities were coal 11 tons and water 6000 gallons. Perhaps the most interesting aspect of this proposal, its great size apart, was the cylinder layout, two each side outside the frames, one above the other, each pair sharing common cross-heads and, between the frames, valve chests. The hand of Samuel Vauclain, Baldwin President from 1919, is evident in this arrangement, which was employed on compound expansion locomotives of his design. The external dimensions of the locomotive would have restricted its field of operation, but because it was intended for one specific function that would not have been considered over restrictive, and although it would have fouled the roof of the 235 yard Conisborough tunnel had that been still in place, Fay's intention was to have it opened out. At the same time as Baldwin's drawing office was busy on the design, back at Gorton Robinson had underway another 2-10-2, this time with only two outside cylinders, 26in by 30in, driving 4ft 8in coupled wheels. Working pressure was 200lb/in^2, but the grate area was not specified. Adhesive weight was 110 tons, all up weight 135 tons. The tender was of modern six-wheel GCR type; capacities were coal 6 tons and water 4000 gallons. Based on tractive effort, at 61715lb the GCR proposal was nominally the more powerful of the two. What makes the latter of particular interest is the Belgian influence. The GCR in Robinson's time employed parallel boilers with Belpaire fireboxes, but here the former is parallel from smokebox only to the second ring, at which point the top tapers steeply upward to a round top firebox, although because of the trailing truck the grate is able to lie much deeper than in the similar, but earlier in conception, Flamme Type 36 2-10-0, which is illustrated in Chapter 10.

Owing even more to the Belgian engine is that visible at left in the painting, a proposal from the Lancashire & Yorkshire Horwich drawing office dating from 1914, for a wide firebox 2-10-0. What the CME George Hughes sought was a locomotive able to haul 1090 tons at 30mph on the level, and in the Type 36, he considered, might lie the answer. Again, the similarity is obvious, except that because of the more restricted British loading gauge, the boiler is domeless, and safety valves are mounted on the left side of the second boiler ring (another drawing indicates a parallel section of smaller diameter with the safety valves on the top line). The L&Y 2-10-0 had a shorter coupled wheelbase, 22.8ft (6960mm), as against 24.9ft (7615mm)on the Belgian engine. Cylinders (4) were 19in by 28in, coupled wheels 4ft 10in, working pressure 180lb/in^2 and grate area 27.5ft^2. Adhesive weight was 80 tons, all up weight 90 tons, tractive effort 53328lb. A six-wheel, short wheelbase tender was indicated; capacities were coal 6 tons and water 4500 gallons.

The other locomotive pictured, the handsome 2-10-2, was a Pickersgill Caledonian Railway project of 1918. This would have had two cylinders 28in by 30in, coupled wheels 4ft 9in, working pressure 200lb/in^2 and grate area 54ft^2. Adhesive weight was 114 tons, all up weight 144 tons, tractive effort 60000lb. Here the boiler was parallel throughout, with wide round top firebox, but perhaps over long, there being 24ft between the tubeplates. The six-wheel tender appears to be the large CR type, capacities coal 5 tons 10 cwt and water 4500 gallons. While one can wonder about its effectiveness, externally it was elegantly proportioned and would have made a splendid sight in the open country of the upper Clyde Valley, working steadily up the northern ascent of Beattock with a long train of mineral wagons, heading for Carlisle, where later at Kingmoor it would meet its Horwich built counterpart, just in from the south. Pity, though, the poor fireman.

The Lancashire & Yorkshire Railway in the Twentieth Century
E. Mason, Ian Allan 1961

A Detailed History of British Railways Standard Steam Locomotives Volume 4
J.Walford/ P. Harrison, RCTS 2008

Heavy Goods Engines of the War Department
J.W.P. Rowledge, Springmead 1948

CHAPTER TWENTY NINE

1929 LIMA LOCOMOTIVE WORKS, USA
WOODARD 2-12-6

In the history of the reciprocating steam railway locomotive, many and varied have been the means of getting coupled wheels around curves, a problem exacerbated by the fact that the heavier and more powerful the locomotive became, the greater the number of driven wheels that were required. Anatole Mallet's compounding (Chapter 26), by supplying high-pressure steam to rigidly mounted cylinders and low pressure to a second set in an articulated frame, was an early approach to the problem which found wide acceptance. Another, which by the 1950s had achieved a high level of sophistication, was the Garratt, in which the boiler unit sat between two articulated engine units. There were others which did well, such as the Meyer and Fairlie (single and double), the Péchot-Bourdon and Mason-Fairlie, while equally many were failures, the Johnstone annular compound just one. Added to which might be gear-drive steam locomotives such as the highly successful Shay, the Climax and Heisler, together with countless logging industry variations from minor builders and the occasional camp blacksmith. On the other hand ten coupled wheels in a rigid frame did not present undue difficulty to designers and the arrangement was widely employed around the world. Side play might be given to leading and trailing coupled axles, the coupling rods having knuckle joints to accommodate movement, while, as in the case of the BR 9F 2-10-0, the centre set of wheels might be without flanges.

This chapter concerns itself with the rigid frame locomotive having twelve coupled wheels, but with cylinders at the leading end only, thus not including the so-called Duplex, which is dealt with in Chapter 36. The first to appear was Philadelphia & Reading 0-12-0T *Pennsylvania*, completed in September 1863 by the railroad's Chestnut Street shops in Reading, works number 52. Initially without road number, in 1871 it became No. 93, having been rebuilt the previous year as 0-10-0. Cylinders were 20in by 26in, wheel diameter 3ft 7in and all up weight 50.16 tons. It was of 'Camel' type with the enclosed driving position forward on the right hand side of the boiler, but perhaps the most interesting feature, shades of Brunton's locomotive, is that it was fired only when stationary and did not carry fuel, an arrangement which was considered sufficient for the short spells of working it undertook as a pusher. The third and fourth pairs of coupled wheels were flangeless, while knuckle joints were located at the second and fifth. No. 93 was scrapped in November 1885. The twelve-coupled locomotive without any carrying wheels was found in small numbers, widely scattered but often long lived. In 1912 the Austrian State Railway, then kkStB (today ÖBB), introduced Class 269 (post-1945 Class 197), three rack and adhesion 0-12-0T for the Vordenberg to Eisenerz section. Designed by Karl Gölsdorf they carried out the same task for more than 60 years. The first, fifth and sixth axles had sideplay, which combined with knuckle joints and a two-part rear section coupling rod with a central pivoting joint and vertical pin joint at either end, imparted sufficient flexibility; a complication, but one which over the years it seems proved trouble free. Another 0-12-0T, a metre gauge wood burner, was supplied by Krauss-Maffei (15722/1930) to the Slavonian Drava Valley railway, No. 81, but after 1949 worked the steeply graded line at the Orahvica stone quarry, where by 1970 it had been plinthed. Two further metre gauge twelve-coupled rack and adhesion tanks, in this instance with a pair of trailing wheels, were built by Esslingen in 1954 for the Argentine General Belgrano system, Nos.100-101; for curves of 120m (adhesion) and 250m (rack) they boasted the refinement of flange lubrication. From 1912 the 1067m gauge system in Java ran a fleet of 28 2-12-2T by Hanomag (18) and Werkspoor in Holland (10). Although early use on the heavily curved Preanger Highlands line caused excessive wear on the leading coupled wheel flanges, they subsequently had lengthy careers elsewhere (F1002, Hanomag 6813/1913, survives at the Ambarawa railway museum on Java). Following the earlier Austrian Class 269, in 1939, to meet increased demand for iron ore, Floridsdorf outlined an enlarged rack and adhesion locomotive for the Eisenerz line, in the form of a 2-12-2T. Two were constructed under German direction (Floridsdorf 9100/1941 and 9101/1942), DRB 97 401-402 (post-1945 ÖBB 297.401-402). Although they were extremely powerful, the earlier 0-6-2 and 0-12-0 tanks were always preferred. Taken out of stock in 1968, 297.401 latterly had seen little use, while its classmate had not worked for 20 years, having been retained at Knittelfeld workshops as a source of spares. A long term operator of twelve-coupled locomotives was Bulgaria, with three series. There were 10 two-cylinder compound 0-12-0T by Hanomag (9991-10000/1922), Bulgarian State (BDZ) Nos. 4001-4010 (after 1936, 45.01-10). Cylinder stroke was 700mm, diameter 620mm HP and a massive 900mm LP; although successful, after 1945 they were converted to simple expansion with 620mm diameter cylinders and Lentz valves, remaining active until the end of the 1960s. The other Bulgarian engines were two groups of 2-12-4T, 12 two-cylinder engines from Ciegielski in Poland (201-212/1931), BDZ Nos.4.501-512 (after 1936 46.01-12) and 8 with three cylinders by BMAG, Berlin (11794-11801/1943), Nos.46.13-20. Happily, their impressive appearance may still be enjoyed, 46.03 having been restored to working order in October 2015. A 2-12-0 tender locomotive was André Chapelon's SNCF 160 A 1, his complex six-cylinder compound rebuild of the Paris-Orléans four-cylinder 2-10-0 No.6030 (SACM, Belfort 6130/1910). Although work began before World War 2, trial running did not take place until after. It was an experiment only, Chapelon in this instance seeking high thermal efficiency at low speeds (a design which it is accepted does not fit the 'cylinders at leading end only' criterion). Of the same wheel arrangement was Gölsdorf's elegantly proportioned four-cylinder compound kkStB 100.01 (Floridsdorf 1966/1911), designed to work all forms of traffic over the south Austrian Tauernbahn. The outbreak of war in 1914 caused the cancellation of an order for a further nine, following which it was decided that ten-coupled locomotives would be adequate. 100.01 was exhibited at the transport exhibition at München in 1925, but withdrawn three years later and cut up. It was not without influence, being the inspiration behind the Württemberg Class K (DR 59º) four-cylinder compound, successful freight locomotives 44 of which were built by Esslingen 1923-1924, DR Nos.59 001-044. By the end of World War 2, examples could be found in Hungary, Yugoslavia, the Soviet Union and, appropriately Austria. The class had seen regular use there during hostilities moving coal over the Semmering to Italy and it was on those slopes that the last, 59 029, by then numbered ÖBB 659.29, finally ceased work on 15 October 1957.

We return now to North America, where the problem of maximising power at the rail was approached rather differently, the rigid frame twelve-coupled locomotive overshadowed by the more flexible Mallet articulated. But in the 1920s there was still a problem with the Mallet, in that the bulk of the leading engine unit with its large compound cylinders had poor tracking qualities limiting maximum speed to about 25mph, for which reason it was unsuited to medium and long distance main line freight haulage. Seeking a solution, the Union Pacific Railroad in conjunction with Alco as builder, introduced rigid frame 4-12-2 No. 9000 in April 1926, testing of which confirmed the ability to move the 125 vehicle load of the Mallets at greater speeds and on half the specific fuel consumption. The prototype was followed over the next four years by a further 87, the largest three cylinder locomotives ever constructed. Another builder thinking along the same lines was the Lima Locomotive Works. The company, best known perhaps for its Shay geared locomotive, was responsible also for the introduction of the so-called Super-Power type, beginning with the 2-8-2 No.8000 of 1922, tested on the New York Central, and establishing itself with the 2-8-4 No. A-1 (Lima 6883/1925), which preceded a first order for 25 from a NYC subsidiary, the Boston & Albany. The Lima design team, led by W.E. Woodard, at the same period was also considering a superior alternative to the 2-8-8-2 Mallet. This gave rise to the 2-12-6 arrangement pictured here. A design study, it was intended to demonstrate how one set of driving wheels and two cylinders could

Its day's work done and fully coaled ready for tomorrow, Gölsdorf 0-12-0T 197.301 is put away for the night at Vordenberg, 31 May 1965. Floridsdorf 2090/1912, kkStB and BBÖ 269.01; DRB 97.301; ÖBB 197.301. Fitted with Giesl ejector 1956; withdrawn 1979; preserved at Eisenbahnmuseum Strasshof, near Wien.

be dispensed with and a six-wheel trailing truck provided sufficient to carry a 151ft² grate area firebox serving a free-steaming large diameter boiler. To the observer, perhaps the most startling feature was the location of two massive 32in by 32in cylinders well ahead of the smokebox and in front of the leading carrying wheels. Woodard's aim was to reduce the adverse effect of piston thrusts on large two-cylinder engines by means of what he described as "unitary machinery support." In this, he brought closer to the centre line in a single casting cylinder saddle, slidebars and valve gear supports. The outline drawing (below), dated 1928, lacks detail, but does indicate 5ft 3in diameter coupled wheels with 27ft 6in between leading and trailing axles (30ft 8in on UP No.9000). Woodard stated that there was nothing in the design which did not have "a sound basis in development already done or by comparison with existing practice."

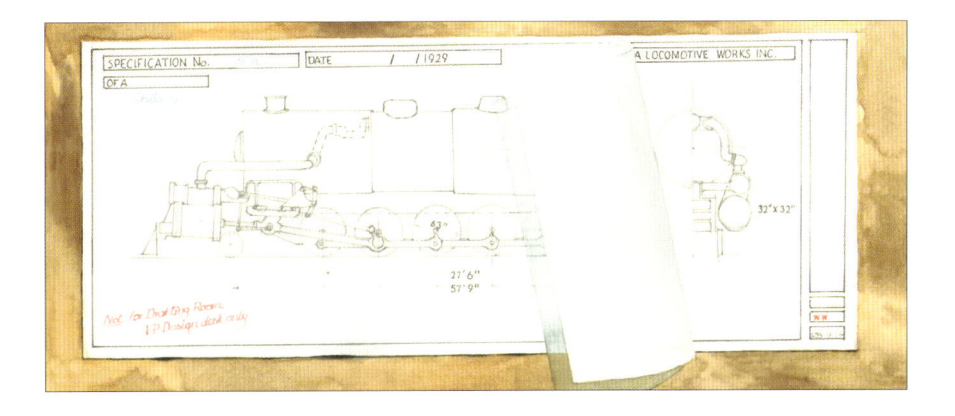

Lokomotive-Athleten
A. Giesl-Gieslingen, J O Slezak 1995

Lima, The History
E. Hirsimaki, Hundman Publishing 2004

Trains & Travel
March 1952 (Blueprint by D P Morgan: Lima steam locomotive projects)

Locomotives in Profile Volume 2
B. Reed (Ed.) (Union Pacific 4-12-2)

CHAPTER THIRTY

1930 LONDON & NORTH EASTERN AND LONDON, MIDLAND & SCOTTISH RAILWAYS, UK

LNER Doncaster and LMS/Beyer Peacock Bo-Bo (Diesel-Electric)

Speaking to the British Association in 1881, Sir Frederick Bramwell (1818-1903), at the time President of the Institution of Civil Engineers, predicted the reciprocating steam railway would be superseded in no more than fifty years. Perhaps his opinions were coloured by the fact that he had been chief draughtsman and manager at John Hague's Cable Street foundry (Chapter 24) when Lord Dundonald's exotic 0-2-0 and the 0-4-0 *London* were assembled, at which period also Daniel Gooch was serving an apprenticeship under him. In the event, although new steam locomotives were constructed commercially for use in Britain until 1964, he was not far out, World War 1 in particular having given great impetus to the progress of the internal combustion engine. He was, however, by no means the first to predict the demise of steam. In 1825, before the railway age had properly begun, a writer in The Fingerpost regaled the reader thus, on the subject of rail travel (in part); "I must ask him to indulge his imagination with an excursion some twenty or thirty years forward in these regions of time; when the dark, unsightly, shapeless machine that now offends him, even in idea, shall be metamorphosed into one of exquisite symmetry and beauty...a machine that may regale his nostrils with exhalations, not from pit-coal and train-oil, but from some genial produce of the earth, whose essence may be extracted at insignificant cost...and its fragrance left on the breeze...which may delight his ear with the concord of sweet sounds." This of course was pre-*Rocket* and external styling, while train-oil was evil smelling animal fat. (The writer was wide of the mark in respect of fragrant exhalations – one recalls first generation BR diesels and the thoroughly objectionable fumes that filled closed-in stations: a prescient piece, nonetheless). First attempts at internal combustion were made almost 200 years before the railway age, a subject well documented, but for our present purpose we are not required to reach back further than 1894, when Priestman Brothers of the Holderness Foundry in Hull fitted the firm's two-cylinder double acting vertical marine oil-engine to a four-wheel chassis mounted on standard gauge rail wheels. The engine almost certainly was the smaller of the two versions then being produced, of 30bhp at 300rpm. These incorporated elements of the 1881 patent held by Etève and Lallement, the engines perhaps more properly described as of Priestman-Etève type. A photograph from the James D. Priestman Collection has been much reproduced, purporting to show this pioneer locomotive, which was tried on Hull & Barnsley Railway trackage at Alexandra Dock, but the writer is certain it does not. In his opinion what is shown is a fully developed inspection trolley, while the light flat bottom rail, open shuttered windows on the building behind, and appearance of the young man are not at all suggestive of this country. Perhaps it was a souvenir of a continental visit, Priestman having involvement with development there and trials such as those at Meaux, France. In the event, the company did not pursue railway applications and it was Ruston & Hornsby who produced the first four commercially successful examples, 18in gauge locomotives with Hornsby-Akroyd oil-engines for the Woolwich Arsenal. From the beginning of the 20th Century several makers, some established, others new, began to produce oil and petrol engine locomotives in numbers, a process massively advanced by World War 1. Most, though, were of narrow gauge, and amongst the earliest of any size, for standard gauge, were twenty 0-4-0 petrol locomotives with mechanical transmission built by Manning Wardle of Leeds (1867-1876/1915 and 1945-1954/1918) for the War Office. Intended to haul trains near the front, but proving unreliable, they were quickly restricted to shunting duty. As for the British main line railway companies, in the decade following the end of World War 1 there was little interest in adopting the diesel (or petrol) locomotive, although railcars were looked upon more positively; pre-Grouping the NER and GCR, for example, employed the type.

It was the LMS in 1927 which could be said to have opened the door to diesel traction for main line companies, management having discovered that 50% of goods locomotive hours were taken up shunting. Furthermore dedicated shunting locomotives passed long periods in inactivity, during which coal and water often would have to be replenished, a two-man crew remaining on duty. A locomotive which could be single-manned and simply switched off when not required, even stabled overnight at its place of work, was obviously an attractive proposition. Thus in November 1932 the first diesel shunter built for and by a British main line company was completed at the LMS Derby Works, a conversion of a 0-6-0T, LMS No. 1831 (Vulcan Foundry 1363/1892, MR Nos.1999 and 1831). A six-cylinder 400hp Davey Paxman engine (later derated to 300hp) in a new body was mounted on the original frames and wheels, while the hydraulic transmission was by Haslam & Newton of Derby. Crude and unreliable, during 1940 converted into a mobile generating unit identified as MPU 3, it nonetheless had suggested what might be possible. The LMS' next step was to order seven diesel shunters with mechanical transmission and one, by Armstrong Whitworth, with electrical. Most significant was a ninth, by Hawthorn Leslie/English Electric, also diesel-electric, initially loaned but later purchased. LMS No.7079, it established the form still be seen today on the British rail network, though in greatly reduced numbers, as Classes 08 and 09. The aforementioned were designed for shunting, but in 1931, even before these first experimental shunters had arrived on LMS metals, Beyer Peacock had drawn up two diesel-electric proposals intended for the company. The Manchester firm remained fully committed to steam, in particular the successful Garratt, but by that date it had noted the growing interest in diesel rail traction, these proposals being an early response. Probably they were unsolicited, but even if they were, they were not taken up. Of 0-4-4-0 wheel arrangement, they would have had two sets of 3ft 3in diameter wheels on a 7ft 6in wheelbase; length over buffers was 34ft 6in and length of body 28ft 4in. Entry was by central door at either end from a railed platform, and as will be seen the overall appearance closely resembled the three Metropolitan Vickers/BTH shunters supplied to the Ford Motor Company at Dagenham in 1932 (No.1 today is on the Kent & East Sussex Railway, a significant survivor). The author has no information as to Beyer Peacock's intended power unit or other details.

The story of the abandonment in 1935 of electric operation between Newport and Shildon is well known, as is that of the NER proposal for main-line electrification from York to Newcastle and probably on to Edinburgh. In the first instance it was the severe downturn in export coal traffic following World War 1 which brought about the decision to return to steam traction, but it had the result of leaving surplus to requirements the ten 0-4+4-0 (LNER description) locomotives which hitherto had handled the traffic. A co-operation between NER Darlington and Siemens Bros., nine were completed in 1914 and the tenth in 1919; they carried the numbers 3 to 12. As traffic dwindled through the 1920s and the full fleet was no longer required, Nigel Gresley put to the LNER Board in July 1928 a proposal to convert one example into a diesel-electric locomotive with a 900rpm 1000hp engine by Beardmore of Glasgow, retaining the four 275hp English Electric motors which would be driven by a generator supplying 1500V dc. As before, length over buffers was 39ft 4in, but weight had risen from 74 tons 8cwt to 90 tons. Intended to haul 1000 ton coal trains on the southern end of the LNER main line, the project was abandoned on several grounds, not least of which was the fact that Beardmore concluded a satisfactory engine installation could not be achieved. Figures were prepared to show the saving in annual operating costs compared with steam would amount to £875, but no saving in wages for crew was indicated, single manning not being envisaged. Here LMS and LNER meet just south of York station, the secondmen exchanging waves, very likely of mutual commiseration.

The British Internal Combustion Locomotive 1894-1940
B.Webb, David & Charles 1973

Beyer Peacock Locomotive Builders to the World
R.L. Hills/D. Patrick, Venture Publications 1998

Locomotives of the LNER Part 10B
RCTS 1990 (Railcars and Electric Stock)

Railway World
November 1980 (J. Brookman; Gresley's Main Line Diesel)

CHAPTER THIRTY ONE

1932 HARLAND & WOLFF, IRELAND
4-6-0-0-6-4 (Diesel-Electric)

Founded in April 1861 by E.J. Harland and G.W.Wolff of Hamburg, the company which bears their names achieved world renown as a builder of large ships, merchant and naval. Most famously, over time, it constructed all seventy of the White Star Line passenger liners, including the *Britannic*, *Olympic* and of course the *Titanic*. Today it functions chiefly serving the business of offshore renewable energy, but it has had involvement in two other forms of transport, air and rail. In 1936, under the Short Brothers & Harland title it entered the aircraft industry, and around 1930, under its own name, rail. Already establishing a reputation as a builder of large marine diesel engines, it became the sole UK licence holder for the two-stroke diesel engines made by the long established Danish company Burmeister & Wain. The seven locomotives designed and built by Harland & Wolff were known as the Harlandic type, and although only two were identical, all were powered by Burmeister & Wain engines. Against Order No. 8252, the first took to the rails in 1933, a 5ft 3in gauge 2-2-2-0 (1AA) powered by a four-cylinder engine with a rating of 270hp at 850rpm, a Harland & Wolff main generator powering two Laurence Scott axle-hung traction motors on the centre and rear axles. Overall length was 28ft 7½in, wheelbase 12ft, wheel diameter 3ft 7in, weight in working order 33.2 tons and maximum speed 50mph. Initially Belfast & County Down No. D1, in 1937 it was renumbered 2 without the letter prefix. When the B&CDR became part of the Ulster Transport Authority in 1948 it was allotted No. 202, but although continuing at work for another three years it never carried the new number. For much of its life it hauled a pair of six-wheel carriages on the short branch from Ballynahinch Junction, 17¾ miles south of Belfast Queen's Quay terminus on the main line to Newcastle, to Ballynahinch itself, 300ft above sea level and the highest station on the railway. As was the case with early diesel locomotives generally, it was temperamental, and in order to alleviate this tendency, as a matter of routine it went each month to the Queen's Quay shops. Even so, helped by the fact it was single-manned, in its first year a saving over steam of £806 was estimated. On withdrawal in May 1950, No.2 was placed in store, then the following year returned to Harland & Wolff, which removed the centre axle, making the wheel arrangement 1A, putting it to work on the sharply curved rails around the shipyard. Obviously useful, it was re-engined in 1959, after which it continued at work until cut up in 1969. In appearance, it was rather like a small steam tank engine, what appeared as a nicely lipped double chimney disguising the exhaust. In 1934, under Order No. 2503, H&W completed its second locomotive, a six-coupled 0-6-0 with a 150hp four-cylinder two-stroke engine, SLM two-speed constant mesh gearbox and cardan shaft drive to the leading axle. Built to standard gauge and numbered 7057, this was one of the group of early LMS shunters referred to in the previous chapter. Length was 25ft 4½in, wheelbase 12ft, wheel diameter 3ft 2in and maximum speed 10mph. In January 1945 it was returned to H&W, given a new 225hp engine and regauged to 5ft 3in, following which it became NCC and UTA No.22, before being scrapped in 1965. The third locomotive, six-coupled, was built in 1935 to 3ft 6in gauge for the Sudan Government Railways, No. 400. It had the 190hp at 1200rpm B&W TR4 four-cylinder engine with a Bostock & Bramley four-speed gearbox and cardan shaft drive. In 1938 it was fitted with a 225hp TR6 engine. Length was 25ft 1in, wheelbase 12ft and wheel diameter 3ft 3½in. At the same period Harland & Wolff's designers and drawing office were busy preparing outlines for main line diesel locomotives, which were offered to railways at home and abroad; they included, for instance, a 5ft 6in gauge 1200hp 260-062 (1`C-C1`) aimed at India and a 2450hp 244-442 (1`BB-BB1`) for an unidentified railway.

The fourth locomotive was a very early example of a twin-bogie main line diesel-electric, built under Order 10170 and completed in 1937. To 5ft 3in gauge, it had a 500hp at 825rpm engine and two Laurence Scott traction motors on the inner axle of each four-wheel bogie, making the wheel arrangement 220-022 (1A -A1).There was a full width cab with a sloping front at one end, behind which the narrower body permitted bi-directional vision; its general appearance was somewhat reminiscent of the BR pilot scheme Type 1 diesels, although it was much smaller. Overall length was 36ft 5½in, bogie wheelbase 7ft and wheel diameter 3ft 7in. Paid for by instalments, it became B&CDR No. 28. Though trouble prone it was used on a variety of duties and kept at work by Harland & Wolff, which saw it as a useful test vehicle for future diesel-electric designs. However, its unsatisfactory performance was a source of friction between maker and railway, which returned it to the former in December 1944, receiving in payment £2500. Hired to the NCC between 1947 and 1951, it also worked under the same arrangement for the Great Northern Railway Board at Grosvenor Road goods yard, Belfast, similarly from October 1958 for the Ulster Transport Authority and finally Northern Ireland Railways. Having worked for five different railway operators carrying the same number and running over the same tracks, it ceased work in 1969 and was scrapped four years later. The second locomotive of 1937 was a 330hp 0-6-0 diesel-mechanical shunter, hired the same year to the NCC, which identified it as Class X No. 17. Employed in Belfast yards, successful and popular, it was purchased by the railway in 1941, later passing to NIR. Withdrawn in the spring of 1966, it was eventually cut up around 1970. 1938 heralded the appearance of H&W's largest entry into the field, two 104 ton 5ft 6in gauge 2-8-2 (1`D1`) twin cab locomotives each with two 450hp at 800rpm TR8 engines, Brown-Boveri generator and four Laurence Scot 250hp axle-hung motors. Overall length was 49ft 11in, wheelbase 37ft and driven wheel diameter 4ft 7½in. Buenos Aires & Great Southern Railway Nos. CM 206 and 207, they suffered the familiar early problems associated with fuel admission and burnt piston rods. CM 207 was damaged beyond repair by fire in October 1941, but CM 206, provided it was not loaded beyond 300 tons, worked reasonably well and remained in service until 1945. The firm's last railway locomotive was considerably smaller, a 0-4-0 with a 225hp at 1200rpm TR6 engine, SLM four-speed gearbox and jackshaft drive to side rods. Overall length was 23ft 4½in, wheelbase 8ft and wheel diameter 3ft 7in. Weight was 28.31 tons and maximum speed 20mph. It was hired to the NCC over 1945-1946, running as No. 20, and later purchased by the UTA it ran as No. 16 until withdrawn around 1965. In passing, it is worth mentioning that Harland & Wolff was not unfamiliar with the steam locomotive, having constructed replacement boilers, in 1945-1949 overhauling all but three of the fifteen NCC Class W 2-6-0s and over the years 1977 to 1984 the preserved GNR V Class 4-4-0 No. 85 *Merlin*. Additionally, the NCC Derby-built WT 2-6-4 tank engines of 1947-1950 were safely delivered on to Irish soil by means of the company's floating crane.

The subject of the painting was an early foray by Harland & Wolff into diesel railway traction, dating from 1931, but fascinating in that it was submitted, under H&W Reference D.3514, to the Great Western Railway. Apparently unsolicited, it was not dismissed out of hand by Swindon, which subsequently engaged in correspondence under its reference 92470, allotting the file number 96665. The maker described it as '460 064 passenger locomotive' (2`CC2`), the GWR as '1600-2200 H.P. Main Line Express Diesel Electric Tractor' ('tractor' was a commonly employed term). Power was to be provided by two 800hp engines each direct coupled to a dynamo, with electric drive through six non-bogie axles. Continuous horsepower was estimated to be 1600 at 550rpm and maximum 2200 at 750rpm. All up weight was 150 tons, wheel diameter (bogie and driven) '3ft 6in (approx.),' maximum tractive effort 51000lb and estimated cost £26000. What really stirs the imagination is a typewritten note at the foot of the outline diagram, obviously entered at Swindon, which reads: 'Designed for "Cornish Riviera Ltd." (see Corres.) Makers estimate this tractor would replace two "King" Class Locos. and effect a working economy of £3400 per annum after first 2½ years.' The Great Western had a forward looking attitude in respect of diesel railcars, but in that of main line locomotives eventually searching elsewhere for alternatives to steam. Here it is seen on trial, about to call at Bath with a Swindon to Bristol stopping train, the Harland & Wolff badge prominent (but carried only by B&CDR D1; the other six H&W locomotives instead had a small plate displaying the word Harlandic).

BackTrack, July 1995
(M. Rutherford; Sages are not Fixers – Science, Invention and Dr Diesel)
The British Internal Combustion Locomotive 1894-1940
B.Webb, David & Charle 1973
The Belfast & County Down Railway
D. Coakham, Colourpoint 2010

CHAPTER THIRTY TWO

1935 GENERAL ELECTRIC/GREAT LAKES AIRCRAFT COMPANY, USA

Aircraft (High-Pressure Steam, Turbine Propulsion)

Pioneers of powered flight perforce turned to the steam engine, no other form of motive power then being available to them. Sir George Cayley (1773-1857) of Brompton Hall in Yorkshire, a gifted amateur scientist, was perhaps the first individual to understand and describe the basic principles of aeronautics, of lift and control. He foresaw a great future for aviation, writing in 1809; "I am perfectly confident, however, this noble art will soon be brought home to man's general convenience, and that we shall be able to transport ourselves and families, and their goods and chattels, more securely by air than by water, and with a velocity of 20 to 100 miles per hour. To produce this effect it is only necessary to have a first mover, which will generate more power in a given time in proportion to its weight, than the animal system of muscles." The core of the problem he had grasped, namely of achieving an acceptable power to weight ratio. As someone of an enquiring mind, interested in scientific advance, one suspects he would have been aware of Trevithick's Penydarren experiment in 1804, although perhaps unsurprisingly, it had not suggested to him the concept of rail transport (later, in 1825 and 1837, he took out Patent Nos.5260 and 7351, for a 'New Locomotive Apparatus' and 'Apparatus for Propelling Carriages on Common Roads or Railways'). As early as 1807 he had planned a steam engine suitable for an air craft (probably a dirigible airship of his design). Of 1hp, it would have had a single-cylinder and a weight of 163lb. William Samuel Henson (1812-1888), born in Nottingham, a lace manufacturer and inventor, between 1825 and 1847 took out ten Patents, most related to machinery associated with lace making, one (8849 of 1841) simply to 'Steam engines' and one, which earned him his place in aviation history (9478 of 29 September 1842) to 'Apparatus and machinery for conveying letters, goods, and passengers, from place to place through the air.' What was proposed was quite remarkable, a large monoplane, having tailplane and rudder, 150ft wing span, with a steam engine powering two four-blade pusher propellors and enclosed cabin for passengers and 'merchandise,' but, once again, ambition had got ahead of technology. Henson was then in Chard, Somerset, where also was another gifted aviation pioneer, John

Stringfellow, the two men for a time collaborating on the testing of models, clockwork and steam powered. None of these early efforts achieved manned, controlled free flight, nor were they intended to. The same applied to Hiram Maxim's giant 'First Kite of War' which he demonstrated along 1800ft of 9ft gauge rail tracks at Baldwyn's Park, Bexley, in 1893. It had two light weight gas fired 180hp steam engines designed by Maxim himself, driving two twin-blade propellors of 17ft 11in diameter.

In the 20th Century alternative forms of power suitable for aircraft, and the debilitating effect of World War 1, led to a decline of interest in steam, although it was still considered. The US Navy Department by 1923 had become unhappy with the unreliability of the widely used Liberty petrol aircraft engine. It was achieving only 72 hours flight time between maintenance periods, each of which took up 300 man hours at a cost of more than $600. George W. Lewis, Executive Officer of the National Advisory Committee on Aeronautics (predecessor of today's NASA), on the other hand did not see steam as widely applicable. His Committee had done considerable experimental work on steam power, but to date met with only partial success, although he considered it might be of use in airships. But steam, he admitted, was "the apex of efficiency" and its "thorough reliability under practically every condition makes it a fertile field for ongoing experimentation." The year 1933 saw what remains to date the only manned, controlled flight by a full size steam powered heavier than air craft, an adapted Travel Air 2000 sports biplane. W.J. and George Besler, sons of the Central Railroad of New Jersey's Chairman, had developed a boiler based on patents acquired from the defunct Doble Steam Motor Company. The power unit fitted to the aircraft was a 90hp vee-twin compound, the cylinders stroke 4in, bore 3in HP and 5½in LP. The monotube boiler worked at 650lb/in². On 20 April, at the US National Aeronautic Association's San Francisco Bay field, W.J. successfully demonstrated the machine, making only a short flight because the amount of oil fuel carried had been deliberately limited to keep down weight. On the ground, he showed how the engine could be instantly reversed. Those present remarked on the lack of noise, the only sound the whirring of the propellor. Sadly, the brothers did not follow up their success in the air, the engine being placed in store (25 years later the US Navy fitted it to a picket boat for experimental purposes).

At about the same time the General Electric Company was keen to promote the steam turbine as a prime mover both in the air and on the ground. In respect of the former, about 1930 it entered into an agreement with the Great Lakes Aircraft Company of Cleveland, Ohio to design a steam turbine power unit and the airframe in which it would be installed. Great Lakes, formed in 1929, was producing a light sport biplane, the 2T-1A, and in 1932-33 completed the sole prototype XP2S-1 and XSS-1 single engine flying boats for the US Navy. Unsuccessful, they were abandoned after a few trials and it would seem unlikely the company would have had the facilities and expertise to produce a totally new design able to accommodate the boiler and turbine installation. Popular Science magazine, October 1931, contained a short article on the project, informing its readers that construction was about to begin under the direction of retired US Navy aviator Captain H. C. Richardson. He is shown with a model of what was suggested to be the aircraft, a high wing twin-engine land plane, but it has always been understood the intention was for it to power a flying boat, which would be better able to accommodate the installation. The author has redrawn unaltered the published schematic (below, left), which clearly outlines the hull. From information available it suggests a single turbine and propeller was intended, with the boiler in the commodious hull. In respect of the painting, he accepts it is conjectural, although possibly coincidentally, what is shown in the schematic is very similar to the late S-series Sikorsky flying boats of that era. It will be seen that the wing is attached sufficiently high above the fuselage to provide clearance for the propeller. The boiler was of the La Mont type working at 1029lb/in² with a superheat value of 540°C. The unit would 'generate 2300hp', optimum operational height was 5000ft, efficiency 23% and average fuel consumption 9.5 ounces per hp. It is believed the boiler and turbine unit was statically tested, though never installed in an airframe.

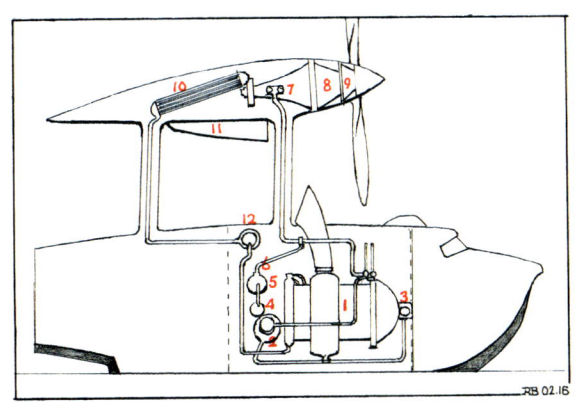

In regard to surface transportation, the steam turbine electric locomotive pictured above was one of a pair, single-ended, constructed by General Electric, emerging from the Erie erecting shop on 3 April 1939. Of 2`CC2` wheel arrangement, they were the first US steam turbine locomotives, but despite being painted as Union Pacific Nos. 1 and 2, in the full company style, they remained the property of GE, which dubbed them Steamotive. Overall length of each unit was 90ft 10in, driven wheel diameter 3ft 8in, weight in working order 265 US tons, working pressure 1500lb/in² (boiler of oil-fired, water tube flash type), fuel capacity 3593 US gallons and water 4782 US gallons. Each rated at 2250hp and geared for 110mph running, the intention was for the UP to run them through from Chicago to Los Angeles hauling twelve heavyweight Pullman cars. This did not happen, as trials revealed a variety of problems, in particular icing of the condenser units, although some fascinating early publicity films suggested a new era had dawned. The pair also toured the US, before continuing testing on the Northern Pacific and New York Central, until in January 1942 returning to Erie, by then painted plain black (as shown). The Pennsylvania Railroad briefly considered leasing them to assist moving heavy wartime traffic on the Indianapolis Division (between that city and Louisville, Kentucky), but fuel oil supply difficulties caused the idea to be abandoned and the two Steamotives were cut up within months.

Steam in the Air
M. Kelly, Pen & Sword 2006

Lokomotivbau und Dampf-Technik
W. Stoffels, PawlakVerlag GmbH 1991

Black Gold-Black Diamonds The Pennsylvania Railroad and Dieselization Volume 1
E. Hirsimaki, Mileposts Publishing 1997

CHAPTER THIRTY THREE

1940 SOUTHERN RAILWAY, UK
Bulleid 4-6-0

It is scarcely possible to write anything new about Oliver Bulleid and his time as CME of the Southern Railway, such has been the coverage of his works, but it is possible to shuffle the vast amounts of published information and revisit some of the less discussed aspects. Prior to the retirement in October 1937 of his predecessor, R. E. L. Maunsell, the chief draughtsman Percy Bollen, under the direction of the Chief Electrical Engineer, Alfred Raworth, was outlining main line electric locomotives of several different wheel arrangements, Bo-Bo, 1`Bo-Bo1`, 1A-Bo-A1 and Bo-Bo-Bo. At that period they would have been of only limited operational value, although of course not long after, a large 1500hp Co-Co electric locomotive, SR No. CC1, was constructed at Ashford, followed by two further examples. Bulleid was supportive and directly involved in their design, but primarily he was driven by steam. A priority was the provision of new locomotives for the heavy boat trains between Dover and London, over a hilly route with a restricted loading gauge, and the long distance expresses to the West of England. On 31 March 1939 Bulleid received Board approval to construct ten, although design work had been ongoing since January the previous year, an initial proposal being a three-cylinder 4-6-2, quickly rejected in favour of a 2-8-2, a wheel arrangement to which he was attached, no doubt the result of his experience with the type under Gresley on the LNER. The first 2-8-2 outlined was an impressive machine, not streamlined or 'air smoothed', for which twelve sets of drawings were made up until March 1939. There were three cylinders, outside 19in by 30in and inside 20½in by 26in, boiler pressure 220lb/in^2, grate area 50ft^2, coupled wheels 6ft 3in and maximum axle load (on second coupled axle) 19 tons. A six-wheel tender would have carried 5 tons of coal and 5000 gallons of water. The author wishes this had been constructed, but having a leading pony truck it was not acceptable to the company's Civil Engineer. He did agree to a revised version with the leading carrying and coupled wheels in a Krauss-Helmholtz truck, but limited to two locomotives on a trial basis only, this in turn not being acceptable to Bulleid. Also in March 1939 some work was done on a 4-8-2 layout, but now the time had come again for the three-cylinder 4-6-2, the first of which, No. 21C1 *Channel Packet*, emerged from Eastleigh Works in February 1941. The story of the resulting Merchant Navy Class and the later lighter Pacifics has been told often, from many different points of view.

Although the Southern has always been looked upon as primarily a passenger railway, one sensibly committed to the electrification of its extensive suburban network, it did of course carry goods. In the London area the load was heavy and challenging to work, the trains forced to share trackage with intensively timetabled, fast accelerating electric multiple-units. Fortunately the company had a fleet of fifteen Maunsell three-cylinder Class W 2-6-4T built in three batches at both Eastleigh and Ashford Works in 1932-1935, well proportioned and competent locomotives. Also to hand were the Urie LSWR tank engines turned out from Eastleigh immediately prior to the Grouping, four Class G16 4-8-0T and five H16 4-6-2T, the former mainly intended for hump shunting at the new Feltham Yard, but with the latter additionally employed on cross-London transfers. Away from the capital the goods workings were less well provided for, the only recent design being the Maunsell Class Q, a modestly proportioned classic British inside-cylinder 0-6-0 (of which arrangement more in the following chapter). Twenty were constructed at Eastleigh in 1938-39, but even so the Southern remained short of goods locomotives for medium and longer distance services, a situation exacerbated by the outbreak of war in September 1939 (this had created a pool of spare passenger engines, but not sufficient to cope with the growth in goods traffic). A second order for a further twenty was cancelled, but even had it been carried through it would not have brought with it great benefit, for although the class was generally useful and like all Maunsell engines reliable, its haulage capability was severely restricted by lack of boiler capacity. Late in 1940 Bulleid had No.531 fitted at Eastleigh with his favoured Lemaître blastpipe and wide diameter chimney. This did improve steaming, to the extent that the entire class was similarly altered (although ironically it was further improved on seven engines, which from 1955 had the Lemaître replaced by the BR Class 4 plain blastpipe and chimney). Bulleid therefore sought and obtained Government authorisation early in 1941 for forty new goods engines, Class Q1, turned out from Ashford and Brighton Works between June and December the following year. More of Class Q would have satisfied the Operating Department, but he was certain something better and more powerful could be provided within the maximum axle load permitted by the Civil Engineer (matching the Q Class). Within that restriction his aim was to fit the largest possible boiler and provide a thoroughly modern front end to achieve a free-running engine. Boiler pressure was 230lb/in^2, grate area 27ft^2, cylinders 19in by 26in, wheel diameter 5ft 1in, maximum axle load 18¼ tons (centre axle) and weight in working order 51¼ tons. The tender carried 5 tons of coal and 3700 gallons of water. They were numbered C1 to C40 in Bulleid's unique adaption of the German system of identifying wheel arrangement, and proved a great success. Much has rightly been made of their ability to pull almost any load that was hung on the drawhook, the one weakness being that although well provided with brakes, steam on the engine and vacuum on the tender, they had to be carefully applied due to the overall light construction. Light construction it had to be, largely to accommodate the generously proportioned boiler, but also because of wartime material shortages; 'Austerity' had become an underlying theme to all activities, the 'air-smoothed' Pacifics notwithstanding, of which these new engines were perfect exemplars. As his son, H.A.V. Bulleid wrote (see sources); "footplate and splashers became archaic anachronisms and were jettisoned enthusiastically." In addition, conventional casing plates following the shape of the boiler could not be used as the shortages had meant the insulation material employed was Idaglass, a non-conducting material, which while effective, was incapable of carrying a load. Instead, the plates were made of thin steel and attached to frame pieces mounted independently of the boiler, the resulting external form illustrated by the accompanying photograph (above) of No. C1 as displayed at the National Railway Museum, York. Withdrawal began in February 1963 with C28, by then BR 33028 and ended in January 1966 with 33020 (C20) and 33006 (C6), despite which the latter remained active for a further four months. The author, travelling from Waterloo to Datchet in August 1965, was snapped out of a reverie at Staines when his train stopped alongside 33006, which was engaged in shunting. As it stood immediately outside his carriage window he was startled to see, stamped on the tender axle box covers, the initials SE&CR. He makes no apology for stating his liking for these engines, which on one level were thoroughly ordinary, the classic inside-cylinder 0-6-0 yet again, but on another were like nothing seen on British rails before or since. They were not arrived at directly, as before the final layout was confirmed in mid-1941, 2-6-0, 2-6-2 and 4-6-0 (pictured; drawing No. W4018, dated 23 April 1940) arrangements had been looked at. The originals have not survived, but fortunately John Click, who served as Technical Assistant to Bulleid, made copies, from which, although little detail is shown, it is possible to see in outline what was proposed. The 4-6-0 would have had three-cylinders, the two outside ahead of the smokebox centred over the bogie, and the inside inclined beneath (a layout very like that of the Pacifics and one might surmise the same valve gear arrangement). The coupled wheelbase at 15ft 9in was 9in less than that of the Q1, but total wheelbase considerably longer at 27ft 6in. Coupled wheel diameter was not shown, but the drawing suggests the same 5ft 1in. A notable visual difference was the use of the existing Maunsell Class N 2-6-0 boiler, with, as it is outlined, conventional cladding. One can only remark it was fortunate this was not proceeded with; it would have been an indulgence and nowhere near as good as the Q1.

Railways South East, Winter 1991-92
P. Atkins (More Light on the Bulleid 4-6-2s; also other Bulleid designs)
Bulleid of the Southern
H.A.V. Bulleid, Ian Allan 1977

CHAPTER THIRTY FOUR

1943 LONDON, MIDLAND & SCOTTISH RAILWAY, UK
Coleman Class 2F 0-6-0

If ever a locomotive type deserved a medal for long and meritorious service it is the humble British inside-cylinder 0-6-0, which for a century, almost throughout the entire steam age, carried out the same task, that of moving goods. The last British Railways steam locomotives to work from Scottish sheds were two members of Matthew Holmes' NBR Class C (LNER J36) BR Nos. 65288 and 65345, both withdrawn in June 1967, while in the north-east of England the considerably larger and more powerful NER Class P3 (LNER J27) remained active for a further three months, doing the work it had always done, moving coal the short distance from pit to port. The last three, Nos.65811, 65855 and 65879 were withdrawn simultaneously on 9 September of that year, just eleven months before the end of all everyday steam operation on British Railways. What is notable is that four of the five were to the end equipped only with engine brake and non-adjustable three-link coupling, an illustration of the reluctance of Britain's railways to invest in improved wagon stock and freight train operation (touched upon in Chapter 28), the odd one out being J36 65345 which latterly at least was vacuum brake and screw coupling fitted. In fairness, in respect of short distance coal haulage, an exception perhaps might be made, bearing in mind the primitive non railway-owned loading and unloading facilities to be found at either end of the journey, with which modern high-capacity wagons were unlikely to be compatible.

At the lower end of the power scale, in classes 2 and 3 (BR classification), the LMS handed over to British Railways in January 1948 a total of 2180 inside-cylinder 0-6-0 tender locomotives. Unlike the LNER and SR, the LMS never had any engines of this type above power group 4, but within that it had no less than 772 engines of Derby design, 192 of them pre-grouping and 580 post, the last two not being turned out until as late as 1941. In Class 2, there were 209 Midland engines by Kirtley and Johnson, one of them a double-frame veteran of 1870,

BR 58110, which survived until 1951, and 121 London & North Western by F.W. Webb, the oldest group, the 4ft 5½in 'Coal Engines,' dating back to 1873. The others were the so-called 'Cauliflowers', vacuum fitted engines with 5ft 2½in coupled wheels which were frequently employed on passenger duties, the most notable being the Penrith – Keswick – Workington services. A feature of these engines, and many from other companies, which strikes the observer is the poor protection provided to the footplate crews, and it is remarkable that they were prepared to accept it for as long as they did. The author recalls wondering at the feelings of the pair on the exposed footplate of the now preserved J36 BR 65243 *Maude*, as it drifted tender-first down the steep grade from Dalmeny Junction with the South Queensferry branch goods one summer's day in 1960, when as is so common around the River Forth, everything was enveloped in a dense, cold, clammy sea mist. Minimal coverage was a feature of the other LMS 0-6-0s from pre-grouping companies which survived into the BR era. From the Lancashire & Yorkshire came a small group of 25 Barton Wright 4ft 6in engines, but the largest single group of Class 2 engines, a reflection of the enormous amount of short distance traffic handled around the dense concentration of mines and heavy industry in the central belt of Scotland, came from the Caledonian Railway, a company which made a fine distinction between mineral and goods working (even for a time painting the locomotives concerned black and green respectively). Designed originally by Dugald Drummond, they were later built in batches with minor changes under Smellie, Lambie and McIntosh, to a total of 244 and how useful they were may be seen from the fact that all but six survived into BR ownership. As late as 1958 134 remained in stock, but at the beginning of 1963 the total was down to 16, the last six being taken out of use in November of that year – well into the diesel age. In the more powerful Class 3 category, the MR contributed 398 of three classes, one with 4ft 11in wheels and two with 5ft 3in, the LYR 282 of two, by Aspinall and Hughes, the Furness Railway six engines of one class (one, BR 52494, retaining the original Pettigrew round top firebox and five having the LYR Belpaire type), the Highland Railway seven of one class (extinct by 1952) and the Caledonian 122 of three series by McIntosh and Pickergill.

On the LMS the search for a more modern and efficient design, versatile and able to run easily at over 50mph, began with a potential replacement for the numerous Midland/LMS Class 4, which regularly saw passenger service, often on quite heavy excursion trains. Bearing in mind the success of the Class 5 Horwich 2-6-0, thoughts turned to a tender version of the Stanier two-cylinder Class 4 2-6-4T, but its route availability was felt to be too restricted by the operating department and for lack of an alternative, construction of small batches of the 0-6-0 continued (15 were added in 1937, 20 in 1939, eight in 1940 and two, BR 44605-06, in 1941). At the end of 1932 some consideration had been given to a variant of the existing 4F 0-6-0 with a new taper boiler, and a return to this was made in 1943 with the coupled wheel diameter reduced to 4ft 11in. The highly competent T.F. Coleman, who as Chief Draughtsman was responsible for both Derby and Crewe drawing offices, and his team, with the support of the then Chief Mechanical Engineer, C.E. Fairburn, were not simply seeking greater efficiency, they were energetically seeking ways to save weight and material. It might be said they were 'doing a Bulleid'. E.S.Cox recalled (see sources); "...to the dustbin with running plates, fall plates, splashers and all the clutter of 100 years of previous design." The first result of these efforts was outlined in drawing DD 3688 of 1943, for a Class 4 0-6-0 with 4ft 11in wheels and 225lb/in² boiler pressure, which would have had an innovative application of bar frames, wide firebox, and Allan valve gear. It was not pursued and the following year a reversion was made to the 2-6-0 wheel arrangement, a tender version of the Fairburn Class 4 2-6-4T. This, too, was set aside, but it led to the well-known Ivatt Class 4 of 1947, a thoroughly modern design, 162 of which were constructed up to 1952 (BR 43000-43161). Little thought was given to the Class 3 power group, although drawing DD 3526 of 1941 proposed placing a taper boiler on the 5ft 3in variety of Midland 3F, uninspired to say the least, but probably it was considered unnecessary in view of the fact there were to be new-build Class 4 and 2 engines. The search for a new Class 2 began in 1934, a drawing prepared at Euston (EU 390) outlining a 0-6-0 with two 16½in by 26in inside cylinders,

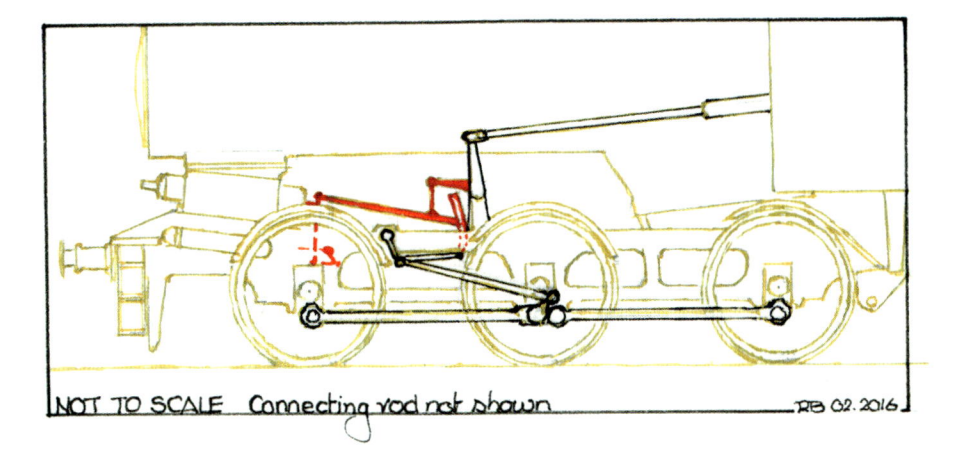

Arrangement of Walschaerts valve gear on the Coleman 2F; return crank and rod outside, expansion link, radius rod and combination lever inside. An additional rearward rod links return crank rod and expansion link.

5ft 0in wheels, a 200lb/in² boiler and 15.5 ton maximum axle load, but there the matter seems to have rested until 1943 when it was updated at Derby (DD 3682), the difference just a 1 inch reduction in wheel diameter. At this point the Coleman team sprang into action, producing two outlines the same year, DD 2714A and DD 3711. An inside-cylinder 0-6-0 was once again envisaged, but bar frames, wide firebox and outside/inside Walschaerts valve gear were specified (Chapter 10). The two drawings differed only in cylinder dimensions (16in by 26in and 16½in by 26in respectively), wheel diameter (4ft 8½in and 4ft 11in) and weight (maximum axle loads were 14 tons and 15.7 tons). The second of the two is pictured here and apart from the features noted above, the round-top firebox is surprising at this stage of LMS history. It will be seen also the boiler has very shallow taper; 4ft 6in diameter at smokebox, it increases to 4ft 9in on the top line. Boiler pressure was 200lb/in², grate area 25.2ft², tractive effort 20390lb and factor of adhesion 5.02. The tender is a cut down WD eight-wheel type, and the forerunner both of the last Ivatt and BR standard designs; capacity was 5½ tons of coal and 3500 gallons of water. In the end, the nominally less powerful Ivatt 2-6-0 of 1946 filled the Class 2 vacancy, but it is interesting to note that during the early stages of its design, an alternative without the leading pony truck was considered in parallel (DD 3771 of 1944). The provision of bar frames and the layout of the valve gear resulted in an inside-cylinder locomotive with working parts hardly less accessible than those of one with them outside. A final point is that what is illustrated has been referred to commonly as a proposed Class 4, but the Derby weight diagram clearly identifies it as Class 2. Probably the reduced chimney and dome height occasioned by the high pitch of the boiler, required to fit the wide firebox above the wheels, make the locomotive appear more powerful than it truly is.

Locomotive Panorama Volume 1
E.S. Cox, Ian Allan 1965

British Railway Steam Locomotives 1948-1968
H. Longworth, Oxford Publishing Company 2005

CHAPTER THIRTY FIVE

1946 SOCIÉTÉ NATIONALE DES CHEMINS DE FER FRANÇAIS, FRANCE

Chapelon 152P 2-10-4

C.R.H. Simpson, in his contribution to Ransome Wallis' encyclopaedia (see sources), was scathing on the subject of compound expansion as applied to the steam railway locomotive, describing it as "an enthusiasm out of touch with reality" and that its supporters frequently "failed to reveal the initial and upkeep costs." He also made the valid point that the advantages brought through superheating did much to negate those claimed for compounding. He did concede that results in France, where fuel was often of very poor quality, were of a "high order," and that there was a case for its employment in low speed, heavy haul articulateds of the Mallet type, where, in earlier applications, supplying high-pressure steam by way of flexible connections was problematical.

In Europe, and in locomotives produced within its boundaries for export, compound expansion was widely applied, in particular to small, narrow-gauge examples of the Mallet and Meyer types, having begun with the little Bayonne – Biarritz tank engines (Chapter 26). Compounding in Britain has already been briefly discussed in Chapter 7 and touched upon elsewhere, but in this chapter the focus is on France, a country in which, as E.S. Cox has written, it became in the 20th Century "almost a national religion," and it is certainly the case it remained so until the end of steam. This was despite the introduction from 1945 of the American 2-8-2s which became SNCF Class 141.R, more than one thousand of which were supplied and proved well suited to post-war conditions. World War 2 had severely damaged France's railway network and the sensible decision was made that a programme of electrification should be introduced, with the consequence, given the presence of the American imports and some requisitioned German examples, that the large scale production of new steam locomotives became unnecessary. To an extent what was produced was simply a continuation of work started before 1939. The 318 141.P four-cylinder 2-8-2s, an improved development of the PLM type, were constructed in batches from 1942, while the Nord Region 4-6-4 express engines had been conceived before the War. The story of André Chapelon's transformation of Paris-Orleans Pacifics into a series of 4-8-0s is well-known and hardly requires repeating, other than to note that the changes substantially increased maximum indicated horsepower and at the same time markedly reduced coal consumption per drawbar horsepower hour. Perhaps his best known work was his reconstruction of the unhappy three-cylinder simple 4-8-2 No. 241.B.1 (pre-SNCF, État 241-101) of 1932, so prone to failure and derailment that in 1936, pending a decision about its future, it was put to use as a stationary boiler at Achères depot. Chapelon decided on almost total reconstruction, retaining chiefly boiler, wheels, some motion parts and tender, but although also staying with the three-cylinder arrangement, as would be expected he introduced compound expansion. What emerged in 1946 was No. 242.A.1, a 4-8-4 able to generate 5500hp in the cylinders. It might be described as a modern incarnation of Edouard Sauvage's very fine Nord 2-6-0 No.3.101, later 3.395, of 1887. No. 242.A.1 demonstrated the ability to restart 635 tonnes (625 tons) on a 1 in 70 upgrade without difficulty and maintain 100km/h (62mph) up 1 in 155 with 856 tonnes (830 tons). One might choose to wonder, however, how it would have performed if arranged as a thoroughly modernised three-cylinder simple. In 1942, the chief SNCF engineers responsible for mechanical design, Renevey and Poncet, had decided that all future high power locomotives were to be three-cylinder compounds, but it was too late, only one of Chapelon's proposed designs ever getting under way. Initially having six-cylinders, following on from the experimental 160.A.1 (Chapter 29), it evolved into a three-cylinder 2-10-4. At the end of the War there was an urgent requirement for heavy-haul freight locomotives in north-eastern France and an order for 100 2-10-4s was placed with Forges et Aciéres de la Marine et d'Homécourt at St. Chamond, only to be cancelled when in 1952 the decision was made to electrify between Valenciennes and Thionville. As is well-known, at least one set of cylinder blocks had been cast. The accompanying painting hopefully gives an idea of its majestic appearance, and one cannot but wish it had taken to the rails, although how it might have performed must remain an unanswered question. Cylinders were two outside 660mm by 760mm LP and one inside 590mm by 760mm HP, boiler pressure 2.2kg/cm² (312lb/in²), grate area 6m² (65ft²), weight in working order 150 tonnes and maximum speed 110km/h. Drawings show it with the curious number 152.01.1, but this was outwith normal SNCF practice, and it is widely considered the class would have run as 152P.

Despite decisions made earlier, the last, great flowering of the French compound was a solitary four-cylinder 4-6-4, Marc de Caso's magnificent No.232.U.1, known to enginemen as 'la Divine', which the author was fortunate enough to see once at Paris-Nord. In 1938, under de Caso's direction, a group of eight high-power express locomotives was to be constructed, four three-cylinder simples (232.R) and four four-cylinder compounds (232.S). Construction of the eighth, originally to have been 232.R.4, was delayed as it had been decided to alter the design to direct drive steam turbine of the Ljungström arrangement, with the new identity 232.T.1. Assembly was begun at the works of Société Alsacienne, but shortly after it was overrun by advancing German forces with the result nothing further was done until the end of hostilities, by which time de Caso had decided on the form in which it appeared in 1949 from the works of Corpet et Louvet at La Courneuve, now numbered 232.U.1. It could without difficulty accelerate a train weighing 582 tonnes (641 tons) from level at 103km/h (64mph) up 4km at 1 in 200 to 108km/h (67.3mph) at the summit, developing an output of 4000 indicated horse power, while between heavy repairs it covered 160130km (99500 miles). It is interesting that despite the fact by then SNCF management considered steam passé de mode, it was this engine that was chosen, specially prepared, to pose beside the delectable Audrey Hepburn for a scene in the 1956 film *Funny Face*.

It is perhaps not inappropriate at this point to say a final word on British compounding. William Stanier (later Sir), in his 1941 address to the Institution of Mechanical Engineers, discussed the difficulties associated in accommodating a large four-cylinder compound within the British loading gauge, the chief of which was that of providing sufficiently generous bearing and crank dimensions. His view was that in practice this could not be done and that any thermal gain would be more than counteracted by mechanical loss. A pencil drawing emanating from Derby in November of the same year outlines a 6ft 9in driver streamlined Pacific having a double Kylchap exhaust, poppet valves and four compound expansion

Les deux divines, Audrey Hepburn and Marc de Caso's tour de force; painting based on a promotional still for the film Funny Face *(1956).*

cylinders, 17in by 26in HP and 25in by 26in LP. It is highly unlikely, however, that it was intended as a starting point for future development, but more to illustrate the point Stanier made in his speech. The statement made by E.S. Cox in a letter to the author that "It is a solid fact no serious consideration was given to compounding in Stanier or Riddles' time" is not negated by the existence of this drawing. One possible solution to the problem presents itself, as employed on the two Nord du Bousquet 4-6-4 express locomotives, Nos. 3.1101 and 3.1102 of 1911. In these, the two low pressure cylinders between the frames were staggered, the right hand half-abutting against the front of the left, and although no doubt unappealing to designers in this country, would have permitted the construction of powerful compound locomotives within the constricted British loading gauges, yet having straight frames and generous bearing surfaces. As applied to the two Nord engines, this layout does not appear to have presented difficulty either in respect of reliable running or routine maintenance.

The Concise Encyclopaedia of World Railway Locomotives
P. Ransome Wallis (Ed.), Hutchinson 1959 (in particular pp 312-314)

Railway Reminiscences of Three Continents
G. Vuillet, Thomas Nelson 1968

Les Locomotives à Vapeur Unifiées Volume 2
B. Collardey/A. Rasserie, La Vie du Rail 2002

La Locomotive à Vapeur
A. Chapelon (English edition, G.W. Carpenter), Camden Miniature Steam Services 2000

SNCF Society Journal 67, September 1992
(Unfinished Business – The 152P)

CHAPTER THIRTY SIX

1948 ROMNEY, HYTHE & DYMCHURCH RAILWAY, UK
Hunter 4-4-4-4 (Duplex Type) 15 inch Gauge

When the term Duplex Locomotive is used, it is normally in reference to the Pennsylvania Railroad's group of 87 built between 1942 and 1946, having rigid frames and four outside cylinders, but in fact the arrangement dated back well into the 19th Century, although installed in a different layout and applied for very different reasons. The first example was Robert Wilson of Newcastle's 0-4-0 of 1825, the exact details of which are not known, but which had four vertical cylinders, possibly 6in by 20in, driving on to the rear axle, which was coupled to the leading. Tried on the Stockton & Darlington Railway, it was not a success, but it was purchased by the railway, dismantled and parts retained for further use. In 1862 the builder Gouin of Batignolles, Paris, turned out a class of eight powerful tank engines for the Chemin de Fer du Nord. To the design of the Nord engineer Jules Petiet, they must remain some of the most remarkable and fascinating steam locomotives ever to run on rails. Rigid framed, with two outside cylinders front and rear, the wheel arrangement was (French notation) 01310T (Whyte 0-2-6-2-0T). Maker's numbers 588-595, Nord 437-444, they were also not a success, although they managed to survive until 1878-1883, while for a time three operated on hire to the Réseau de l'Eure. Essentially, each was two single-driver locomotives in one and in a particularly awkward arrangement, the aim of doubling the haulage ability of the Nord Cramptons unrealised. They had Petiet's steam drier with blast led horizontally atop the boiler, before exhausting upward immediately ahead of the footplate. Similarly arranged, but more useful, were his 20 (French notation) 060T (Whyte 0-6-6-0T), again by Gouin, maker's numbers uncertain, possibly 596-605 and 626-635 of 1863 and 1867 (some sources give 655-664 and 685-694), Nord 601-620 (Gouin also supplied two to the Saragossa (Zaragoza)-Alsasua railway in Spain). With the ability to burn very low-grade coal, they cut the cost of operating 600 ton mineral trains by one-third, but once heavier rails had been laid were superseded by more conventional 0-8-0s. Also CCt were the two Saxon state system Class XV HTV (HTV-superheated tank locomotive, compound arrangement), Nos.1351-1352 (Hartmann 3843-3844/1916). Here each pair of cylinders was located back to back in a single block between the two sets of six-coupled wheels, low pressure leading, with Klien-Lindner hollow axles at outer ends giving 37mm sideplay. They were intended for steeply graded lines in the Erzgebirge region, but had short lives and Nos.79 001-002 allotted under the Reichsbahn 1925 scheme were never carried. Within three years they had been withdrawn, although No.1352 for a time served as a stationary boiler at Leipzig. Vauclain and usually tandem compounds had four outside cylinders, but they belong to a different discussion. One class of locomotives perhaps ought to be included because it appeared to belong to the Pennsylvania style of Duplex. PLM (later SNCF) Series 151.A.1-10, they were built by Schneider of Le Creusot in 1932 for working 1250 tonne freight trains Laroche–Migennes–Dijon. They were compounds, low-pressure cylinders leading and inclined high-pressure between the second and third coupled wheels, giving the appearance of divided drive 2-4-6-2, but hidden from view was the inside connection between the two sets of wheels, so that their wheel arrangement was (French) 151 (2-10-2). While in the USA crank axles so arranged would not have been contemplated, in practice they gave no trouble, and the class averaged 130000km annually, with 280000km run between heavy repairs. After electrification of the PLM lines, all ten were moved to Audun-le-Roman depot on the Est Region, where they were well received and worked 2050 tonne freight trains from there to Hargarten-Falck and Écouviez until withdrawn by 1955.

The modern Duplex type, arising out of the growing problem caused by heavy reciprocating machinery, was introduced not by the famous Pennsylvania classes, but by a single 4-4-4-4 on the Baltimore & Ohio Railroad. Class N1 No.5600 *George H. Emerson* and named after its designer, it was constructed at the company's Mount Clare workshops in 1937. In order to minimise the coupled wheelbase (19ft 9in) the second pair of cylinders were mounted behind the rear driving wheels in an awkward location beneath the firebox. To its operators, it was a nuisance, and although on at least one occasion it attained 100mph regaining lost time with a heavyweight Washington to New York fast train, it was withdrawn in 1943. The Pennsylvania Board of Directors authorised the construction of the PRR's first Duplex in August 1937, the design work on a 4-4-4-4 able to match the performance of the new GG1 electric locomotives being undertaken by a committee consisting of company engineers together with representatives of three major builders, Alco, Baldwin and Lima. Construction was undertaken at the PRR Altoona workshops, other than of the massive 77ft 9in long single-piece cast-steel frame, with cylinders and smokebox saddle, which was outsourced to General Steel Castings of St. Louis. By the time No. 6100 emerged early in 1939, it had grown into the giant 6-4-4-6 illustrated in the Introduction to this book. The production Duplex passenger engines of 1942-1946, Class T1 6110/6111/5500-5549, were more modest 4-4-4-4s, which while not lacking in speed and power, were plagued with problems and overtaken by events. In 1948, following a collision with a K4 Pacific, requiring the frame to be straightened and new rear cylinders provided, T1 No. 5500 had the awkwardly located (inside) Franklin Type A poppet valve gear replaced by externally mounted Type B, unexpectedly turning it into a star performer and frustratingly suggesting what might have been. The freight Duplex engines, Class Q1 4-6-4-4 (No. 6130) and Q2 4-4-6-4 (Nos. 6131/6175-6199), built between 1942 and 1945, similarly were capable of great feats of haulage but expensive to operate. PRR returns for 1949 gave cost per locomotive ton-miles as diesel $ 2.67588 and steam $ 5.79656. The cost of operating the T1 was almost 60% higher than a 4000hp diesel-electric A+B passenger unit, and not surprisingly all the PRR Duplex locomotives had ceased work by 1952. On a lesser scale, Alco in 1945 offered a non-streamlined 4-4-4-4 Duplex to the 3ft 6in gauge South African Railways with 5ft 6in drivers, four 16in by 26in cylinders and a 300lb/in² boiler. Rigid wheelbase was 11ft 6in between second and third coupled wheels, suggesting a form of sideplay in the first and fourth. The proposal was not taken up.

Even smaller, considerably so, than the SAR Duplex, would have been the 4-4-4-4 pictured, intended for the 15 inch gauge Romney, Hythe & Dymchurch Railway in Kent, 14 miles in length and some of that double-track; a true railway in miniature and deservedly famous. Today the steam locomotive stock includes eight 4-6-2, two 4-8-2 and one 0-4-0 tender locomotive, all but one, the Pacific No.11 *Black Prince* (Krupp 1664/1937) having been built new for the railway between 1925 and 1931. After World War 2 not only was the earlier idea of freight traffic revived, the proposal being that the RH&DR would transport beach shingle from Romney Sands to New Romney, but also there was the problem to be dealt with that heavy passenger trains chartered by local holiday camps were having to be double-headed. In 1946-48, Harold Holcroft, one-time Technical Assistant to Bulleid on the Southern, at the request of the RH&DR's manager J.T. Holder, outlined straightforward 2-8-2 and 4-8-2 locomotives, the only unusual feature being the use of the US Baker valve gear. For a variety of complex reasons, neither came to fruition, but also in 1948 the company's owner, Captain Howey, approached Ian Hunter, a BR technical assistant at Derby, asking him to design a 4-8-4 which would be capable of hauling 200 tons at 50mph on level track. The result was a handsome machine of most impressive appearance, in published drawings numbered 14 and named *Lord of the Isles*. Mindful of the possibility the railway might be extended, involving gradients of up to 1 in 40, he went further in dramatic fashion, outlining additionally this giant of the 15 inch gauge, which was drawn as RH&DR No.20 *Cinque Port of Romney*. Apart from its size, No.20 differed from the PRR Duplex in employing compound expansion, the two high-pressure cylinders slightly inclined over the leading bogie and low-pressure horizontally mounted between the second and third coupled axles. The author has no information in respect of leading particulars, although the driven wheel diameter would appear to have been the same 2ft 3in proposed for the 4-8-4. In its lineaments the latter was fairly traditional, but the Duplex has an affinity with the original external appearance of Bulleid's Pacifics. Referring to No. 20 as eye-catching surely is an understatement.

Railways South East, Winter 1987-88
(P. Ross; The Ghosts of Romney Marsh)

Black Gold, Black Diamonds, Vols. 1 and 2
E. Hirsimaki, Mileposts Publishing 1997/2000 (change from steam to diesel on PRR including story of Duplex classes)

Chemins de Fer du Nord, Locomotive List 1842-1938
J. Davies, self-published 1997

La Compagnie du Nord-Belge et ses Locomotives
A. Dagant, Editions PFT 2009

CHAPTER THIRTY SEVEN

1987 DEUTSCHE REICHSBAHN, GERMANY
Wendler 2'C (Fireless)

Here we take a considerable leap forward in time though somewhat less so in technology, for what is depicted is the simple fireless locomotive, albeit writ large and in unique form. The fireless has been used primarily at industrial locations on shunting and short distance work, where there is a supply of steam available from stationary boilers and in particular at those where there is a high risk of fire and/or explosion. In essence it is the simplest of locomotives, for although there is a pressure vessel which must be safely maintained, it has few working parts. Furthermore it is cheap in first and running costs, single-manned, has lengthy economic life and is in itself totally non-polluting. Additional to all these advantages, the fireless does not have to carry around a supply of fuel, being best described as an insulated hot water container – a 'thermos flask' – three quarters filled with water and topped up by high pressure steam. Intervals between recharging would be dependant on the demand made upon the locomotive, but charged at the end of the day and left to stand overnight, it would lose only about 25% of its pressure and thus be instantly available for service in the morning.

The first fireless locomotives were intended to haul passengers on street tramway systems, possibly beginning in the USA with the trial in October 1873 of a four-coupled 4 ton 3 cwt example supplied by the Fireless Engine Company. Hauling a single 120-person capacity car (it is not known how many passengers were on board) it covered the 3½ miles from East New York to Canarsie in just under 13 minutes, returning, on an upgrade, in 17. It had been charged to 180lb/in² prior to the start and this appears to have sufficed for the round trip, but although reports suggest the trial was regarded as a success, there was no follow-up. For a time from 1876 the streets of New Orleans were home to a group of eight 2-2-0 fireless designed by Theodore Scheffer, able to pull one loaded car six miles before recharging. That they proved unsuccessful was not so much through any inherent shortcoming, but because of difficulties experienced with the stationary charging plant. The fireless steam tram did achieve some success elsewhere, most notably in the Dutch East Indies, on the 1188mm gauge system serving Batavia (Djakarta) and its suburbs. Between 1882 and 1907 34 were delivered by Hohenzollern of Düsseldorf-Grafenberg to the Niederlandisch-Indische Tramweg

Maatschappij, numbered I-XXIII and 24-34, all four-coupled. They worked this attractive, tree-lined tramway apparently without difficulty until 1933-34, when they and a group of coal-fired tram locomotives introduced in 1921 were replaced by electrification (the system closed in 1964). The first example for Batavia, Hohenzollern 244/1882, was also the first fireless locomotive to be constructed by the company, which became the leading German manufacturer of the type, until it closed down in 1929 producing 398 in total. It was also the first company to complete what was to become the most common version, the industrial shunter. This was 351/1884, a standard-gauge outside-cylinder 0-4-0 for the Skoda works in Plzeň, then in Austria-Hungary. The last in what was by then West Germany was by Jung of Jungenthal, 14099/1970, a large six-coupled engine for ARBED S.A. of Esch, Luxembourg, although production continued in the East. In between, sixteen different German builders had turned out more than 1200, ranging from just two by Freudenstein of Berlin (in 1904) to almost 400 by Hohenzollern. Between 1913 and 1963 the Wiener Lokomotiv Fabrik, Floridsdorf, in adjacent Austria, completed 86, with one further example to the final design by its successor company, Simmering-Graz-Pauker AG, in 1973. A small Hanomag product for underground operation is illustrated in Chapter 25.

Orenstein & Koppel of Potsdam-Babelsberg was a major producer, completing 301 up to 1940, when it was retitled Maschinenbau und Bahnbedarf AG (MBA), only to be severely damaged during World War 2. Afterward, now in the Soviet sphere of influence, it was further retitled VEB Lokomotivbau Karl Marx (LKM), initially producing narrow-gauge and industrial steam locomotives, and from 1954 examples of the new Reichsbahn main line classes. Earlier, in 1952, it began the production of fireless locomotives, four- and six-coupled, which continued until 1961, after which there was a gap until 1969 (243 works numbers were allotted up to 1961 and 63 in 1969, but around 70 lack any detail or listed destination and may not have been completed). The German Democratic Republic was chronically short of fuel, in particular diesel for transport purposes. For this reason, at the beginning of the 1980s it was decided that a requirement for more industrial locomotives could be met by restarting production of the latter-day LKM Babelsberg 0-6-0. This had two cylinders 660mm by 500mm, wheel diameter 1000mm, wheelbase 3600mm, maximum service reservoir pressure 20atm (294lb/in^2) and maximum tractive effort 9400kg (20724lb). No changes were made to what was a sound, serviceable locomotive other than some minor adjustment to the suspension, and a further 202 were added to the German total between 1983 and 1988. Because locomotive construction had ceased at Babelsberg in 1976, the new series was constructed by the Reichsbahn workshops Helmut Scholz at Meiningen (which famously, under DB auspices, continues steam work to this day). The reservoirs were made by the boiler works at Dresden Übigau. The reunification of Germany in 1990 brought a dramatic reduction to heavy industry in the East and soon after rows of almost new fireless locomotives were to be seen standing idle; the last to be completed, work's number 03202/1988, was scrapped after only eight years.

Supplies of good locomotive coal had long been a problem in Germany, and since 1924 attempts had been made, with mixed success, to adapt soft brown coal to locomotive use. 'Braunkohlefeurung' required specialist equipment and was awkward to handle, but such were the post-1945 difficulties in the DDR that the system found its way into regular service, the last locomotive so-equipped, the 2-10-0 52 9900-3 (former 52 4900) being taken out of service on 10 June 1979. In the forefront of the programme had been Hans Wendler (1906-1989), one-time technical director at Meiningen, who following its completion was made responsible for the state-promoted conversion of withdrawn locomotives into stationary boilers for industry. An original thinker, never short of ideas even in retirement, in 1986 he proposed a Gilli-type high-pressure fireless as a means of saving fuel. He suggested that, based on Erfurt, eleven such locomotives could each run between 220km and 480km a day, covering the passenger working Arnstadt-Meiningen, Arnstadt-Ilmenau, Arnstadt-Saalfeld, Meiningen-Eisenach, Erfurt-Nordhausen and Erfurt-Eisenach, a total of 70 trains daily.

The post-1945 DDR standard six-coupled fireless, a straightforward and useful machine. Built at Meiningen in 1984, work's number 03012 spent its working life with VEB Energiekombinat Karl Marx Stadt, Anschlussbahn Küchwald, but is seen here, in steam, at Sächsische Eisenbahn Museum, Chemitz-Hilbersdorf, on 24 August 2007. The number 18 201 is a nice touch by someone with a sense of humour, for it properly belongs to the famous and unique three-cylinder high-speed 4-6-2, the 1961 Meiningen rebuild of the 4-6-6T DR 61 002.

Using a central charging point, 71 tonnes of coal per day would be saved. It was covered by his Patent DD261126A1 of 19 October 1988, but there was never any chance it would be taken up by the DR, electrification now being well established and steam in any form, as almost everywhere, out of consideration. It will be seen that the chassis of the famous Prussian P8 4-6-0 (DR 38) was to be utilised, the boiler to be replaced by a main reservoir with a superheater, saturated steam entering from a secondary reservoir on the right side and superheated exiting into another on the left, thence to the cylinders. There is of course no tender, the five-axle trailing vehicle a second main reservoir (a four-axle version was also drawn). Charging connections were front and rear. Basic dimensions would have been those of the Type 38; other details, such as the maximum pressure are not known, though the water content is given as (leading) 12885kg, (trailing) 65754kg. The scheme would have been impossible to bring to fruition as by that date there would have been few usable Type 38 chassis remaining.

Feuerlose Lokomotiven
K. Pokschewinski, Lokrundschau 2000

Kohlenstaublokomotiven der Deutschen Reichsbahn
D. Winkler, EK-Verlag 2003

Fireless Locomotives
A. Baker/A. Civil, Oakwood Press 1976

POSTSCRIPT

CONTRASTING IMAGES OF THE LAST YEARS OF STEAM

The Stephenson Locomotive Society/Manchester Locomotive Society Ashington Railtour of 10 July 1967 and visits to the Millom Hematite Ore & Iron Company in Cumberland, 1965-1966

Enthusiasts today have much to be grateful for, that on an increasingly intensively worked national railway system it is still possible to enjoy interesting and varied rail tours, but nonetheless it is probably true to say they attained their zenith during the 1950s and 1960s, when BR would even transfer rare and elderly steam locomotives over lengthy distances solely to head up a tour.

The Ashington Railtour recalled here also had the advantage of being blessed by cloudless skies. Commencing at Huddersfield behind Class 5 45428, it ran to York where Jubilee 45562 *Alberta* took over. From there the train was routed via the East Coast main line to Ferryhill, then by way of Leamside, Washington, Pelaw, Gateshead and King Edward Bridge East Junction to Newcastle Central (water stop), following which it ran to Ashington Colliery by way of Heaton, Percy Main, Hartley and Bedlington. The return journey ran via Backworth to Newcastle Central and then up the East Coast main line to York, with a water stop at Ferryhill, the final stretch to Huddersfield behind 45428 once again.

At Ashington, there was a tour of the then vast internal railway system in a train made up of one former LMS and two NER carriages, used on the workmen's service which had ceased in May the previous year. In charge was that rare beast, an industrial locomotive purchased specifically for passenger service; NCB No.39 (R. Stephenson & Hawthorn 7764/1954), it

NCB No. 39

45562 Alberta on arrival

45562 Alberta waiting departure

90

was one of two identical 0-6-0T. Around the Ashington running shed were 17 immaculate steam locomotives, with three under repair in the adjacent workshops and three more stabled at Lynemouth Colliery.

The other extreme is shown here (above), on the opposite side of the country, where a small industrial locomotive is seen working out its last years.

Operated latterly by the Millom Hematite Ore & Iron Company, the appropriately titled Hodbarrow Mines covered a large area on the north side of the Duddon Estuary, opposite Barrow-in-Furness. Life for those employed at the mines even in summer could be harsh, their bleak and exposed nature illustrated by these two photographs taken in the last years before closure in March 1968. The colour image shows Avonside 1563/1908 returning from tipping sand into a disused shaft, indicated by the small bare patch of ground just in front of the locomotive (23 September 1966). The other is a view to the south-west, some very informal trackwork running down to below sea level from where sand had been collected. In the background may be seen the vast sea wall, the Hodbarrow Outer Barrier, which at a cost of £600,000 had been constructed between 1900 and 1905 to protect the mines from flooding (17 November 1965). For visitors like the author, the operation was a time capsule, a fascinating glimpse into 19th Century industrial practices and as was so often the case in those days, the welcome was friendly with freedom to wander at will.

VALETE

THE CULPRIT
BARCLAY 170

In the Introduction we met the locomotive that more than any other fired the author's enthusiasm, Andrew Barclay maker's number 170 of 1875, Callendar Coal Company No.3, already seventy years old when he first became aware of its existence. As second fiddle to its stablemate, No.7, Barclay 1981, then a mere fourteen years in service, its appearances were intermittent, limited to such times as when the newer engine was under repair or boiler washout. Such occasions probably were not warmly anticipated by the enginemen, as the veteran was unable to push as many wagons up the steep gradient from the Falkirk High exchange sidings. Here we see it making hard work of propelling a single, somewhat decrepit example upgrade from the brickworks at Glen to Policy Colliery, which was located on the hill above the LNER main line station and tunnel, the date the first summer of NCB ownership, and the latter still in faded Callendar livery. Barclay 170 had arrived new from Kilmarnock in 1875 resplendent in the maker's favoured green, very elaborately lined in black with white edging lines, the saddle tank bearing the painted title Callendar Coal Company Ltd. No.3, with above, the name *Glenfuir* (Glenfuir House, situated about a mile west of Falkirk High station, close to the junction of the Union and Forth & Clyde canals at Lock Sixteen, was the home of James Potter, one of three partners in the company, the others James Dougal, managing director, and William Hamilton). How No.3 was painted around the time of nationalisation is uncertain, the recollection only that it bore a dull, unadorned green, without number or other identity, but later the letters NCB were applied to the tank sides.

As described in the foregoing Introduction, in 1922 No.3 had gone back to Kilmarnock for an extensive overhaul, happily returning unaltered in appearance apart from the fitting of a new, shorter chimney, which in the opinion of the author was better proportioned visually than the original. On 1 January 1947 it passed into state ownership, to NCB Scotland's No.3 Central West (later Alloa) Area, but remained at Policy until cut up about the time the mine closed in November 1959, having attained the good age of 84. Its partner, No.7, after nationalisation worked at a number of collieries in the region and when scrapped in 1956 was at Kinneil, Bo'ness.

An abiding memory of old No.3 is of one day, when as was his habit in fine weather, meandering slowly homeward from Falkirk High School (Primary), the author arrived at the level crossing over the Slamannan Road, just below the colliery. A steam roller, which had been compressing freshly laid tar on the crossing, moved back at the sound of the engine taking a run at the bank, propelling a short rake of empty wagons, whistling furiously as was normal practice (the driver was unsighted until almost upon the crossing). To his horror, the author noticed the gap between running and check rails had been filled; unaccountably, as the tar had been spread manually, leaving no grooves for the flanges of the wheels. No-one, crossing keeper or workmen, appeared in the least concerned. It quickly became apparent why – the wagons first, then the locomotive, formed them as they passed through the wet tar.